Does My Child Need Help?

Disclaimer

This book is designed to increase knowledge, awareness and understanding of psychological and educational assessments. It is not intended to replace the advice that your own educational psychologist can give you. If you are concerned by any of the issues raised in this book make sure you consult your child's psychologist, who is there to help you.

Whilst every effort has been made to ensure the accuracy of the information and material contained in this book, nevertheless it is possible that errors or omissions may occur in the content. The author and publisher assume no responsibility for and give no guarantees or warranties concerning the accuracy, completeness or up-to-date nature of the information provided in this book.

DOES MY CHILD NEED HELP?

A Guide to Educational Assessments and Interventions

William K. Wilkinson

ORPEN PRESS

Published by
Orpen Press
Lonsdale House
Avoca Avenue
Blackrock
Co. Dublin
Ireland

e-mail: info@orpenpress.com
www.orpenpress.com

Paperback ISBN 978-1-909895-46-1
ePub ISBN 978-1-909895-47-8
Kindle ISBN 978-1-909895-48-5
PDF ISBN 978-1-909895-49-2

Printed in Dublin by SPRINT-print Ltd.

To my late mother, Jane Bradford (1923–2012), for her everlasting creativity, encouragement, joie de vivre, humour, warmth and love.

About the Author

Dr William K. Wilkinson is an educational psychologist specialising in the assessment and treatment of learning and behavioural problems. He has operated a private practice in Galway for the past nineteen years. Prior to that, he completed doctoral training at University of California, Berkeley, Northern Arizona University, and Johns Hopkins University School of Medicine, Behavioural Psychology Department, Baltimore. He was also an assistant professor at New Mexico State University in the Department of Counselling and Educational Psychology.

He is currently an adjunct lecturer in the Clinical Psychology doctoral programme at National University of Ireland, Galway. He is the author of *Research for the Helping Professions* (Pacific Grove, CA: Brooks/ Cole, 1995) and *Straight Talk about AD/HD: A Guide to Attention Deficit/Hyperactivity Disorder for Irish Parents and Professionals* (Cork: Collins Press, 2003). He and his wife Mary have raised three boys, Kyle, Drew and Zane.

Acknowledgments

The following people were instrumental in the completion of this project:

- Ailbhe O'Reilly, commissioning editor, Orpen Press, for seeing the potential in the material.
- Eileen O'Brien, editor, Orpen Press, for her knowledge, dedication and thoroughness in all aspects of the finished product.
- Mary Wilkinson for her support and inspiration throughout.

Contents

List of Abbreviations xiii
Preface xvii

1. **Introduction** 1
   Initial Contact 2
   Psychologists' Qualifications and Training 5
   Who Conducts Assessments? 7
   Preparing for an Assessment: Key Questions 9
   What Do I Say to My Child? 9
   Do I Need to Bring Anything? 10
   What Happens? 10
   How Long Before I Get a Report? 11
   A Parent's View 12
   A Sample Psychological Report 13
   Summary 24

2. **Assessment Methods – Subjective Sources** 26
   Introducing the Assessment 27
   Child Interview 28
   Behaviour Observations 31
   Previous Reports 36
   Parent Interview 39
   School and Home Visit 44
   Summary 48

3. **Assessment Methods – Objective Sources** 50
   Rating Scales 51

Contents

Conners' Rating Scales 52
Brown Attention Deficit Disorder Scale 54
Gilliam Asperger's Disorder Scale 55
Adaptive Behaviour Assessment System 57
Rothwell–Miller Interest Blank 59
Summary of Rating Scales 61
Performance Tests 62
Intelligence Tests 63
Achievement Tests 73
Summary 82

4. **Educational Diagnoses** **84**
Labels – Myths and Reality 84
Cognitive Disabilities/Talents 90
Specific Learning Disabilities 90
General Learning Disability 94
Comprehension Disability 96
Non-Verbal Learning Disability 98
Gifted Children 99
Summary 101
Emotional/Behavioural and Autistic Spectrum Disorders ... 102
Internalising Conditions 104
Externalising Behaviour 107
Autistic Spectrum Disorders 114
Motor and Language Disorders 121
Dyspraxia 121
Specific Speech and Language Disorder 124
Summary 127
A Parent's View 129

5. **Post Assessment – The Report** **131**
Psychologist's Report: Sections and Content 132
Identifying Information 132
Reason for Referral 133
Evaluation Procedures 135
Test Results/Outcomes 136
Behaviour Observations 144

Contents

Parent Interview 145
Teacher Interview 146
Review of Records 147
Summary and Analysis 148
A Parent's View 152
Final Comment 153

6. Post Assessment – Recommendations **154**
Language Exemptions 155
Reasonable Accommodation for Certificate Examination
(RACE) 159
Resource Support 162
Special Needs Assistant.. 171
Home Tuition.. 173
Special Units... 174
Assistive Technology... 181
Disability Access Route to Education (DARE)...................... 184
Further Assessment... 186
Recommendations for Parents 187
Review Assessment 204
A Resource Teacher's Perspective................................... 204
Final Comment.. 206

7. Conclusion.. **208**

References and Contacts **212**

List of Abbreviations

ABAS-II	Adaptive Behaviour Assessment System, second edition
ADD	attention deficit disorder
AD/HD	attention deficit/hyperactivity disorder
AD/HD – HIP	attention deficit/hyperactivity disorder – hyperactive–impulsive presentation
AD/HD – IP	attention deficit/hyperactivity disorder – inattentive presentation
ADQ	Asperger's Disorder Quotient
AP	attention problems
AS	Asperger syndrome
ASD	autistic spectrum disorder
AT	assistive technology
AW	anxiety/withdrawal
BADDS	Brown Attention Deficit Disorder Scale
BAS	British Ability Scales
CCBRS	Conners' Comprehensive Behaviour Rating Scales
CBT	cognitive behavioural therapy
CD	conduct disorder
CELF	Clinical Evaluation of Language Fundamentals
CogInattent	cognitive problems/inattention
cvc	consonant–vowel–consonant
DARE	Disability Access Route to Education
DCD	developmental coordination disorder (dyspraxia)
DES	Department of Education and Skills
DSM-V	*Diagnostic and Statistical Manual of Mental Disorders*, fifth edition

EB	emotional/behavioural
EBD	emotional and behavioural disorders
FULL	Full Scale Score
GAC	General Adaptive Composite
GAD	Generalised Anxiety Disorder
GADS	Gilliam Asperger's Disorder Scale
GAI	General Ability Index
GLD	general learning disability
GP	general practitioner
HSE	Health Service Executive
HI	hyperactive/impulsive
HYP	hyperactivity
ID	intellectual disability
IEP	individual education plan
IT	inattentive type
MDE	major depressive episode
ME	manic episode
ME	motor excess
MR	mathematical reasoning
NCSE	National Council for Special Education
NEPS	National Educational Psychological Service
NO	numerical operations
NVLD	non-verbal learning disability
OCD	obsessive–compulsive disorder
ODD	oppositional defiant disorder
OT	occupational therapist
PB	psychotic behaviour
PO	perceptual organisation
PR	perceptual reasoning
PS	processing speed
RACE	Reasonable Accommodation for Certificate Examination
RBPC	Revised Behaviour Problem Checklist
RC	reading comprehension
RMIB	Rothwell–Miller Interest Blank
RS	reading speed

List of Abbreviations

SA	socialised aggression
SAD	separation anxiety disorder
SEC	State Examination Commission
SGP	spelling/grammar/punctuation
SLD	specific learning disability
SNA	special needs assistant
SP	social phobia
SP	spelling
SP.ED	special education (Department of Education and Skills)
SSLD	specific speech and language disorder
VC	verbal comprehension
WAIS-IV	Wechsler Adult Intelligence Scale, fourth edition
WE	written expression
WIAT-II	Wechsler Individual Achievement Test, second edition
WIATMR	Wechsler Individual Achievement Test – mathematical reasoning
WIATNO	Wechsler Individual Achievement Test – numerical operations
WIATRC	Wechsler Individual Achievement Test – reading comprehension
WIATRS	Wechsler Individual Achievement Test – reading speed
WIATSP	Wechsler Individual Achievement Test – spelling
WIATWE	Wechsler Individual Achievement Test – written expression
WIATWR	Wechsler Individual Achievement Test – word reading
WISC-IV	Wechsler Intelligence Scale for Children, fourth edition
WISCFULL	Wechsler Intelligence Scale for Children – Full Scale Score
WISCPR	Wechsler Intelligence Scale for Children – perceptual reasoning

List of Abbreviations

WISCPS	Wechsler Intelligence Scale for Children – processing speed
WISCVC	Wechsler Intelligence Scale for Children – verbal comprehension
WISCWM	Wechsler Intelligence Scale for Children – working memory
WM	working memory
WPM	words per minute
WR	word reading
WRAT-4	Wide Range Achievement Test, fourth edition
WRATSP	Wide Range Achievement Test – spelling
WRATWR	Wide Range Achievement Test – word reading

Preface

Even though a significant number of families have direct or indirect experience of educational psychologists' assessments, there is a mystique around the assessment process. As a psychologist, a common question I get from prospective clients is 'What do you do?' If more information were available regarding the assessment process, the question would not be necessary.

The main incentive for writing this book is to address the need for clear and detailed information as to what exactly is involved in an assessment. What types of tests are used? What other methods are used to gather information? What kinds of conclusions are reached? What can be done once the problem is clearly specified? The answers to these questions are the focus of this book.

There should no mystery or confusion regarding psychological assessments. There are many excellent references about specific problems, such as dyslexia, Asperger syndrome, attention deficit/hyperactivity disorder (AD/HD) and autism. I have added to the specific category approach with my last book, which was about AD/HD.* Across all specific categories, there is a standard operating procedure as to how assessments are conducted, how psychologists come to diagnostic conclusions, and what help is on offer once a diagnosis is made. Thus, rather than focus on a specific problem, one aim of this book is to list and explain common assessment procedures, how diagnostic conclusions are reached, and what help is on offer if a problem is detected. By understanding the methods and outcomes of an assessment, and removing any misconceptions and mystique, you will know

---

*   William K. Wilkinson (2003) *Straight Talk about Attention Deficit/Hyperactivity Disorder: A Guide for Irish Parents and Professionals* (Cork: Collins Press).

what to expect. Ultimately, you will be more informed as to whether your child could benefit from an assessment.

To help explain the tests used in an assessment and the possible outcomes, this book includes a number of simple line graphs, displaying example outcomes of standardised measures used by psychologists. A graph of test results is a visual X-ray, which anyone can understand. The goal is helping the parents to link assessment results with diagnostic conclusions (e.g. what does dyslexia look like on a graph or X-ray).

In addition, another aim of this book is to correct misinformation about assessments. For example, a common complaint is 'I don't want my child labelled' or 'All the psychologist can do is get my child out of Irish.' These and many other misguided notions will be addressed in the chapters to follow.

What most individuals may not know is that an assessment is often the beginning of a much improved life for the child/student, both at home and school. The child and parents will learn that there may be a clear reason for academic difficulties and that there are other people with similar problems. Testimonies written by parents about the positive impact of an assessment on a child's life are included in the forthcoming chapters. Without understanding a child's personal strengths and weaknesses, parents and teachers are prone to attributing a child's struggles to 'laziness' or simply argue he/she 'needs to try harder'. The results of an assessment can offer a completely different interpretation and help people to move forward and find solutions. There are many types of support; the most common interventions for a variety of problems are discussed in Chapter 6.

An assessment represents a win–win situation for all involved. If the outcomes do not indicate a problem, then you know the original concern leading to an assessment cannot be attributed to a particular cognitive, behavioural or social–emotional deficit. When an assessment does not uncover a problem, this narrows the scope in terms of why the problem is a problem; in fact, maybe the problem is not even a problem (e.g. an assessment can rule out the fear or suspicion that a child has a learning difficulty by giving an objective measurement of the child's learning abilities). These outcomes represent a win. And, if there is a clear problem, everyone wins because once the problem is clearly identified procedures and strategies can be put into place to remedy the issue.

In Chapter 6, one of the strategies for assisting children discussed is the provision of extra teaching support in school. At the time of writing, August 2014, the National Council for Special Education (NCSE) has proposed a new system governing how additional teaching support is allocated (refer to the Resources and Contacts section at the end of this book for further information about the proposal). Essentially, 'learning support' and 'resource support' teachers will be collapsed into one group referred to as 'special education support teachers'. Schools will have a baseline level of special education support teachers and any additional teaching allocations will be based on (a) school profile, (b) results of school tests and (c) number of students with 'complex special educational needs'. It is this latter category that probably defines all of the disabilities discussed in Chapter 4. Since many of the topics in the proposal are relevant to this book, it is important to clarify several points:

- As explained in Chapter 1, there are three types of service providers offering assessments of children: the National Educational Psychological Service (NEPS), the Health Service Executive (HSE) and private practice psychologists. Of these three service providers, the first two are funded through the state and parents do not pay for the assessment. On the other hand, parents who seek private assessments pay for the service. The advantage of a private assessment is that parents do not have to wait months or years before an appointment.

  One rationale for a change in the allocation of support teaching resources is that the current system is unfair because some parents can afford private assessments and therefore can access supports faster than parents who cannot afford a private practitioner's fees. Suffice it to say this is an ethical, moral and political issue about which you can form your own opinion. The NCSE will continue to accept assessments from private practice psychologists; rather, the underlying agenda is that parental financial status should not determine how soon a particular school receives resources, or how many.

- According to the proposal, 'many professionals feel obliged under the current system to label a child as having a disability simply to ensure the school gets additional teaching hours.' Actually, this represents a misunderstanding of the assessment process. As an example, consider a parent inquiring about an assessment for her seven-year-old with suspected learning and attention problems. A psychologist undertaking this assessment would gather information from a variety of sources, both subjective (parent interview, observations of the child and report from school) and objective (tests of cognitive ability and ratings of behaviour at home and school). This information, discussed in Chapters 2 and 3, may indicate a clear pattern regarding a learning problem, attention problem or both. The psychologist will be able to analyse the data and inform the parent and teacher as to the primary issue and what can be done to intervene. Sometimes, as discussed in Chapter 4, nothing significant emerges in an assessment. Or, if a problem is detected, it may not be of enough significance to warrant any additional school support. If a parent's reason in seeking an assessment is to obtain extra teaching support for their child and this support cannot be recommended the parent will be disappointed. A psychologist cannot make a diagnosis simply because a parent or teacher wants one. This would be unethical and unprofessional. The primary motivation for the majority of parents seeking an assessment is to (a) determine if there is a problem, (b) if a problem is found, be able to identify it, (c) measure how significant (mild to severe) the problem is, and, most importantly, (d) outline what can be done about it.
- The NCSE proposal indicates that teaching resources will be allocated to the schools through in-house school tests. It is not clear what school tests will be used and what levels of performance will be linked to support provision. Most parents are familiar with annual standardised school tests (e.g. MICRA-T, SIGMA-T and Drumcondra). It may be that these tests will continue to be used and that if a child's academic progress is below a certain level additional teaching will be provided. In fact, this is already the case, so it is unclear exactly what is different about the proposal in this regard. It should

be pointed out that results on school-administered standardised tests do not yield the same results as the standardised achievement tests used by psychologists and discussed in Chapter 3. That is, a child might perform near the average level of reading skill on a standardised school test, yet obtain a much lower score on a test like the Wechsler Individual Achievement Test, second edition (a test discussed in Chapter 3).

- One final point is that additional teaching resources will be considered when students present with 'complex special educational needs'. It is assumed that students with complex special educational needs will be professionally assessed in order to determine exactly what these needs are. From the proposal, it is not clear if teachers will determine which children have complex needs and how this determination will be made. In any case, if an individual educational plan is required, a psychological assessment will be fundamental to this plan.

Regardless of how the NCSE proposal is implemented, the topics and questions raised in this book remain the same. Psychologists will continue to use the assessment procedures discussed and will continue to diagnose the conditions mentioned in Chapter 4. The main question that you need to consider is, does my child need help? After reading this book, you will be in a far better position to objectively and thoroughly answer this question.

1

Introduction

My work, for the past twenty years, has revolved around psychoeducational assessments. An assessment requires collecting information to determine psychological and educational strengths and weaknesses with the ultimate goal being the development of an individualised educational/behavioural/social programme. The outcomes have great relevance to teaching and parenting, as well as helping children understand their own skills and difficulties. Such knowledge greatly benefits self-awareness and the development of a realistic and positive self-appraisal.

While assessment methods are fairly standard, the interactions with children and adults are always different. Of course there are patterns: similar reactions, similar stories, similar outcomes and similar reports. Yet, within the repetition, there is amazing variability: the nuance of success and failure, the quality of questions from the person being assessed, the unique manner in which the background is presented and the different emotional reactions. After thousands of assessments, my interest is continually maintained by the unknown: what will happen, what will the results indicate, what will parents say, how will they react and what can I do to help?

The impetus for this book is my belief that an educational assessment is a win–win situation. If a problem clearly emerges, then it needs to be acknowledged, pinpointed and remediated. This is a clear win. If no clear issues manifest, then parents or the adult client have one less thing to worry about. This allows the participants to explore other explanations and to problem-solve knowing what problems are not present.

Another impetus is to dispel the obvious misconception that, somehow, an assessment represents a 'punitive' step. In fact, a parent might use the threat of a psychologist's assessment as a negative reinforcer: 'If you don't start studying and making an effort, I will take you to the school psychologist.' As ridiculous as this may sound, it does represent the view of some individuals.

In fact, in an ideal world, every student would undergo an assessment. The assessment would be a child case study, involving standardised testing, observations and developmental history. A report of outcomes and conclusions would be provided to parents and teachers. The assessing psychologist, parents and school staff would meet and develop an individualised instructional/behaviour programme. Imagine each child starting school with knowledge of their clear strengths and some possible areas to monitor. There would be repeat assessments and meetings at the end of every year. Parents would be informed of all outcomes and parents and teachers would be provided with an ongoing plan of support. The reality, of course, is that this is logistically and financially impossible.

This book is devoted to outlining exactly how an assessment proceeds. What actually happens? How does it work? What are the benefits? Some of the beginning elements, such as first contact, are discussed in this introduction. The nuts and bolts of an assessment – the procedures and methods – are the focus of the next two chapters. The outcomes of an assessment are divided into three topics, discussed in Chapters 4, 5 and 6: diagnoses, report and interventions.

INITIAL CONTACT

The initial contact with the psychologist is extremely important. There are different lines of inquiry and many different methods used in assessments. Also, one might have a misunderstanding of what an assessment involves. At the outset of communication the psychologist will explain the process and clarify why the assessment is sought. An initial understanding of the reason a parent seeks an assessment for their child provides the foundation for the remaining procedures. Reasons for an assessment can be communicated in different ways. For example, some parents are aware of the names of common childhood disorders, and they may preface an assessment with a question like 'Does my child have dyslexia or attention deficit/hyperactivity disorder (AD/HD)?' Or, the reason given for referral may be stated in a different manner, such as reports of problems keeping up in school, issues with comprehension or difficulties relating to other children. Personally, I find it useful when parents are specific and make reference to the name of the problem they believe is evident (assuming they know the specific problem they feel applies to their child).

Also, parents and teachers can reference a previous diagnosis. For example, if the child was assessed before, what was the outcome? Is the parent looking for a review to determine the current status of the previous problem? Or, they may state what types of recommendations/services are sought (e.g. exam accommodations, resource support, a special needs assistant, assistive technology or language exemptions).

Sometimes a parent will note an important transition period, for example the child is transferring from primary to secondary school and requires an updated report. In such a situation, the assessing psychologist would be wise to inquire about the findings derived from the first assessment.

Any and all of these comments will help the psychologist to individualise their assessment. There is no one-size-fits-all approach, as there are numerous methods of gathering information. Thus, it cannot be overstated how important it is for the assessing psychologist to select the right methods to address the issue. If the parent and the psychologist do not adequately communicate at the time of initial contact, then the parent may be disappointed with the entire process.

There is a core set of fundamental tools that will be used in most assessments. For example, most educational psychologists will use cognitive tests, namely intelligence and achievement measures. A cognitive work-up is normally the bare bones of an assessment (cognitive tests will be covered in Chapter 4). At the minimum, these tests should take at least 90 minutes to administer, with actual time varying depending on the number of specific tests given, factors specific to the person being tested (age, time required to solve problems, etc.), factors specific to the psychologist (e.g. amount of patience and wait time allowed) and factors specific to the environment in which the person is being tested (interruptions, distractions, etc.).

During cognitive assessment, one subjective data source is observation of the person being assessed. How do they respond to challenging problems? Do they persist or give up easily? Do they reflect or answer quickly and without reflection. What is their level of concentration? Did they lose focus as the assessment continued? Do they interact easily or remain quiet? Do they use any techniques or strategies to facilitate problem solving? For example, when recalling number sequences, do they 'shadow write' the numbers on the desk? There are numerous insights one can glean during the process of completing standardised tests.

In addition, depending on their age, an educational psychologist can engage in an 'interview' with the student. The form and clarity of this interview depend greatly on the ability of the child to answer questions about education, learning, career desires and so on. Their ability to use language to explain and articulate issues are key factors in understanding their perspective. Also, social interactional variables are paramount, such as whether the child is comfortable enough to reveal important details, or has difficulties with conversation and tends to be more quiet and reserved.

If a younger child is assessed, then the interview will focus on information gleaned from their parent. The information needed will depend on the type of assessment. If the assessment is mainly to do with learning and concerns about academic/school skills, the interview is typically brief (e.g. What are your major concerns about learning? What interventions are you looking for?). Typically, a lengthy developmental history is not necessary. On the other hand, if the reason for the assessment is behavioural/social/emotional/medical then the interview process will include structured questions as required. The types of interview and typical questions asked are covered in Chapters 2 and 3.

Another source of information for a psychologist is previous reports from other professionals. Parents may provide assessment reports from occupational therapists or speech and language therapists, medical reports, and reports from other psychologists. The assessing psychologist can then review these reports to ascertain (a) findings and diagnoses, (b) how the child responded to the assessment and (c) key background details.

There are many additional tests and measures which can be included in the assessment. Suffice to say that the inclusion of various tests depends entirely on why the assessment is requested. It would not make sense to test areas that are not of concern (e.g. inclusion of emotional measures when emotional functioning is not an issue). Again, the quality and precision of the initial contact is paramount in guiding the psychologist to selecting the right tests.

PSYCHOLOGISTS' QUALIFICATIONS AND TRAINING

It is important for those seeking assessments to understand how differences in professional qualifications and training relate to the type of assessment service provided. Let's establish a few basic points.

At university level, Educational Psychology is a graduate study or post baccalaureate degree. The Bachelor of Arts/Science degree obtained by students pursuing postgraduate study of Educational Psychology can be in either Education (e.g. as in teacher training colleges) or Psychology. In an Educational Psychology graduate programme, the terminal degree can be masters or doctoral. A Masters of Arts (MA) degree in Educational Psychology is sufficient for some forms of employment, assuming the MA is recognised by the appropriate professional organisation and that experience elements are met. For example, in Ireland, an MA is sufficient for private practice in educational psychology. An MA will also suffice for employment within the Department of Education.

A doctoral degree enables a wider range of career options. With a doctoral degree, one can pursue university positions (e.g. teaching). Also, a doctorally trained educational psychologist should have greater understanding of the technical aspects of assessments; in addition, the longer the training programme, the more experience is garnered, which should lead to a deeper understanding of the entire assessment process. In Ireland, doctoral training (PhD) in Educational Psychology is now more available than it was previously. This is a welcome trend as a therapist's level of training is an important element in determining who you want to conduct the assessment.

The second point is not 'how much training' but 'what type of training' is required. Here lies a topic of some controversy, namely the difference between clinical and educational psychology. It is important to know how differences in training relate to the assessment process. One main difference is that a clinical psychologist's training is not confined to children, but may also include adults. More importantly, the training of a clinical psychologist will include a deeper understanding of mental illness as well as therapeutic training (e.g. forms of psychotherapy). By comparison, an educational psychologist's training is usually oriented to school-age children. One focus for educational psychologists is understanding special needs, such as learning disabilities, behavioural difficulties, coordination issues and social–emotional deficits.

In reading various reports by clinical and educational psychologists, the differences are:

- Clinical psychologists' reports are more likely to include reference to emotional functioning (e.g. anxiety) relative to educational psychologists.
- Educational psychologists' reports usually have more recommendations for teachers due to their background in education.
- In Ireland, clinical psychologists are provided more latitude in diagnosing emotional and behavioural disorders relative to educational psychologists. For example, the Department of Education accepts autistic spectrum disorder diagnoses from clinical but not from educational psychologists.

Department of Education circulars are equivocal on the matter. In some circulars (e.g. 05/01, 08/02), reference is made to 'psychiatrists' and 'psychologists' when it comes to diagnosing emotional and behavioural disorders. The type of psychologist is not specified. In another circular (04/09), 'clinical psychologist' is referenced in relation to certain diagnoses.

There is a certain degree of implicit self-regulation on the part of the assessing psychologist. If the psychologist has basic postgraduate training in Educational Psychology (a Masters degree), then it is unlikely they will have sufficient training to assess certain problems (e.g. AD/HD). This is due to lack of training in the assessment process related to AD/HD or other low-incidence special educational needs. For example, training in DSM (the *Diagnostic and Statistical Manual*, discussed in Chapter 4)) is essential. Briefly, DSM is one common diagnostic system used by psychiatrists and psychologists to identify, through accumulated research, the symptoms associated with a particular disorder. DSM training is not usually part of masters level training in Educational Psychology. However, the DSM is often covered in doctoral programmes so that doctorally trained educational psychologists can diagnose the same conditions first evident in childhood as a clinical psychologist (where DSM training is an essential part of doctoral clinical psychology study).

The take-home point for the parent is the importance of understanding how different types and levels of training influence the assessment. If you are interested in an assessment of AD/HD, the first question is whether this type of assessment is in the repertoire of the psychologist. If so, will their recommendations be accepted by the administrative unit responsible for overseeing special needs allocation (the National Council for Special Education (NCSE))?

Who Conducts Assessments?

Clinical and educational psychologists conduct assessments. Psychological assessment can be accessed through the Health Service Executive (HSE), the National Educational Psychological Service (NEPS) or via psychologists in private practice. In some cases, parents may bring their initial concerns to their general practitioner (GP). The GP may then refer parents to any of the above providers. In the case of private practice psychologists, parents do not need a GP referral to make an appointment with a psychologist.

The Department of Education has a dedicated staff of psychologists who form the National Educational Psychological Service (NEPS). Part of the brief of these psychologists is to conduct assessments within schools. Each primary school has a ratio of assessments to enrolled pupils, which is one assessment per fifty children. As this is a very small ratio, the school has to prioritise the number of children who can be referred to the NEPS. Typically, the needs of children referred to the NEPS are on the significant end of the spectrum. The NEPS also has a panel of psychologists with whom assessments can be carried out. These psychologists usually have other forms of employment (e.g. private practice or university teaching). Psychologists on the NEPS panel receive payment from the Department on a commissioned basis (each completed assessment is paid at a fixed rate).

Finally, there are some psychologists who function mainly in a private practice capacity (self-employed). Again, parents can make direct contact with these psychologists to make an appointment.

Each service has pros and cons. The advantage of assessments through the HSE is that parents might be able to access a multi-disciplinary team, where different professionals have input. Also, interventions can be undertaken through the HSE, such as occupational therapy, speech and language therapy, child psychiatry, psychology or social work. The HSE's service is free, which is especially relevant in the current economic climate.

On the down side, the HSE may require significant time to process a referral (i.e. there are waiting lists). Each discipline within the service can require a separate waiting period. Not all professionals have the same theoretical view, which can lead to differences of opinion about diagnosis and treatment. I find that unless the problem is grave and urgent, the HSE may not be particularly interested in processing the case. When I refer to the HSE, based on my perception of a significant issue, it may be refused on the basis that the problem is not serious.

Most parents who seek assessments do so based on concerns about learning and behavioural problems that manifest in school. The overwhelming majority of these cases do not require HSE involvement. A single psychological assessment may be all that is required to identify the problem and form an intervention plan.

As for the NEPS, one advantage is that the assessing psychologist will visit your child's school. This allows the psychologist to directly observe the child in school and provides the opportunity for a face-to-face meeting with teachers. In the majority of assessment reports I review, the tests used are often confined to those of the cognitive spectrum. As many NEPS psychologists are trained to masters level, the use of cognitive tests for determination of cognitive disabilities is entirely appropriate. Nonetheless, this limits the assessment to a particular domain, and any queries about other disabilities (e.g. behavioural problems) require formal referral (i.e. to the HSE).

As for private practice psychologists, the advantage is that appointments can be made directly with the service provider and waiting lists for private assessments are relatively short compared with those waiting for NEPS and HSE appointments. Private psychological assessments are not free. The fees can vary anywhere from €300 to up to €1,200, depending on the experience and qualifications of the psychologist and the length of time required to collect information. The range of fees may seem excessive but perspective is important, as the fee covers at least a three-hour assessment and full report. With report writing, proofing, printing and packaging (with attached handouts), the total time increases accordingly. Also, psychologists' assessment costs should be considered in line with other professional fees, such as those of accountants, solicitors and medical consultants. If one bases a fee on an hourly rate, imagine the cost of four hours of direct contact with any well-trained consultant.

For parents who cannot afford a private psychologist's assessment and the situation requires urgent attention, there may be alternative funding arrangements. For example, sometimes parents and the school can split the fee, or, in some cases, the school will pay the fee. Furthermore, there may be alternative agencies (e.g. charities) which can provide financial assistance.

PREPARING FOR AN ASSESSMENT: KEY QUESTIONS

Below I discuss the answers to a number of common questions about the assessment.

What Do I Say to My Child?

This question only applies to younger children, as older students usually know something specific about why they are attending for assessment (e.g. concern about their concentration, reading or spelling). For younger children, parents come up with a variety of explanations. They might be quite creative, for example, 'You were one of the lucky children in the school to be picked to do educational games.' Or parents might be more direct and tell their child that a person is going to help them find the best way to improve a certain area, such as reading, maths or concentration. Personally, I believe the direct approach is best for most children as it can lead to a candid discussion about the problem and your child's view of it, and create a collaborative problem-solving effort between parent and child.

At the beginning of an assessment with younger children, the psychologist will overview the types of tasks the child will complete, such as showing them a sample of reading material. They might also show them some of the picture-type tests. Within a few minutes children realise it is lot like school and any fears or concerns evaporate. Sometimes students of any age get teary when they encounter difficulty with particular tasks, such as reading, writing, maths or answering oral questions. With reassurance and a positive attitude, this negative feeling is temporary.

Do I Need to Bring Anything?

The general answer is no, just you and your child. If parents wish, previous reports and documents (mentioned above) can be sent in beforehand via email or standard post. As the assessment lasts for a long period, water and a snack are advisable. A younger child might want something small to eat while waiting during the parent meeting.

What Happens?

Initially, the child completes the tasks in a separate office. For younger children, parents may wish to wait in an adjoining room. In many cases, parents will leave and come back when the child is finished the standardised testing sequence.

What parents do during the child assessment is completely their choice. The least advisable strategy is for the parent to remain in the office during the testing, as this changes the dynamic (e.g. parents may try to help the child with the task, give hints or provide feedback). Of course, the psychologist would request the parent to refrain from any of these actions. Sometimes, if children are apprehensive, the parent can stay for a few minutes than gradually move into the waiting room. Or the door can be left ajar, so the child only loses visual contact with their parent.

Once the child testing aspect is completed, the parent meeting follows. This can sometimes take as long as the child assessment. The child will ideally wait and watch movies or use a device of interest (portable game, mobile phone, etc.). Of course, if the child has difficulty waiting and interrupts often this is a valuable behaviour observation. If parents bring other siblings to the appointment, it may be wise for one parent to entertain the children while the other parent meets the psychologist.

How Long Before I Get a Report?

The turn-around time between the conclusion of the assessment and receipt by parents of a report can vary. Some parents have informed me that they have waited up to a month, and, in rare cases, considerably longer. This is true across all service providers.

As I can only control my report writing, the typical time to receive a report from me is one week. This is the case in 99 per cent of assessments. However, there are times when the report may be delayed. For example, in some situations, during the parent consultation, a problem emerges that was not anticipated. For example, if a child was assessed for dyslexia and a different problem emerges, such as AD/HD, the psychologist may require parent/teacher rating forms to be completed. The report cannot be completed until the rating forms are received, so the responsibility is on the parents/teachers to collect this information as soon as possible. Once received, the report can be finalised and sent to the parents.

A PARENT'S VIEW

Below is the view of Ursula, who had her son Adrian assessed.

Adrian is seven and he is my second child. He has one older brother (aged twelve) and two younger brothers (aged five and six). We live in an Irish speaking area. I have no Irish, but my ex-husband is a fluent Irish speaker.

When Adrian started in the local national school, which is a Gaelscoil (Irish-speaking school), the teacher felt there was something 'wrong'. Another teacher wondered if he was depressed. At home, he was extremely difficult; he would not sit still and never lasted at any one activity, even television. He could not do homework as he could not concentrate for any length of time. Every morning was difficult; Adrian was difficult to wake, did not want to get dressed, and was reluctant to get into the car for the short drive to school. There was lots of shouting and crying and we were all very stressed out. He went to school with his head down and looking cross and angry.

I mentioned my concerns to the teacher and principal and was told that it could be years before Adrian was assessed. I made an appointment with a private psychologist. The results indicated severe dyslexia and attention deficit disorder. After the assessment, we decided to change school. The following year, Adrian started attending a non-Gaelscoil. He is now flourishing. He settled into the new school and straight away his behaviour changed. Now he is the first up, eats breakfast and is ready for school without tension. He is happy and agreeable. The new school is much farther away but it is worth it to see Adrian happy and no longer angry or frustrated. He still has difficulties in school, but we can manage. My older son continues in the Gaelscoil and is doing well. Getting Adrian assessed was the best decision I made as he now goes to school with a smile on his face.

This scenario captures how an assessment can have a profound impact on a child's education and the entire family unit. Ursula knew something was wrong, as most parents do, and took action. The result was a complete change in Adrian's feelings about school. Whereas he was previously frustrated and angry, he is now happy and content. The finding of severe dyslexia is particularly relevant. Since dyslexia is a fundamental problem with learning languages, particularly the underlying phonics of a language, this outcome would explain why an Irish-medium education was so frustrating for Adrian. Obviously his older brother, who is not dyslexic, is able to cope and dually process separate languages; Gaelscoil education does not pose a problem for him.

In her note, Ursula mentioned the word 'assessed' and that Adrian would be seen through the NEPS, but this could take up to four years. She could not sit by and passively watch her son being miserable. Fortunately, she had the means to circumvent the long waiting lists of the public system and so she made the decision to obtain a private assessment. As mentioned earlier, if a situation is deteriorating and you cannot afford a private psychologist's fees, inquire about financial assistance. The least advisable approach is to take no action at all.

A Sample Psychological Report

What does a final report look like? Below is a sample report where the student required an updated assessment to access various supports and services.

The evaluation methods mentioned in the example report will be covered in Chapters 2 and 3. The conclusion, and many other potential assessment formats and conclusions, will be outlined in Chapters 3 and 4. Greater detail about sections of the report will be the basis for Chapter 5. Finally, the recommendations mentioned in this example report, as well as numerous other recommendation, will be fully covered in Chapter 6.

****

CONSULTANT PSYCHOLOGIST'S REPORT

Name: Tina Murphy
Address: 12 The Street, The Estate, Town, Co. Anywhere
Date of Birth: 20 July 1996
Age at Testing: 16 years, 10 months
Date of Evaluation: 6 June 2013
Date of Report: 7 June 2013
School: Anyschool
Year: Fifth

Reasons for Assessment

The reasons for the consultant psychologist's assessment are:

- Updating Tina's cognitive profile; her initial assessment was in 2008
- Providing recommendations based on the obtained profile.

Evaluation Procedures

Cognitive Tests

- Wechsler Intelligence Scale for Children, fourth edition (WISC-IV)
- Wechsler Individual Achievement Test, second edition (WIAT-II)
- Wide Range Achievement Test, fourth edition (WRAT-4)

Informal Measures

- Behaviour observations
- Parent/client report

Cognitive Outcome

Figure 1.1 provides standard scores for all cognitive tests. Table 1.1 provides a brief description and interpretation of the scores in the chart.

Figure 1.1: Summary of Tina's Outcomes

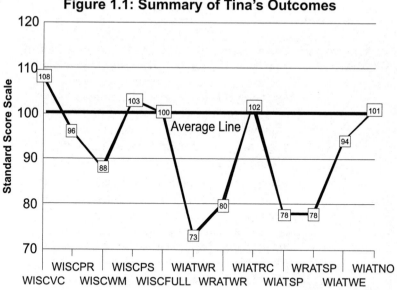

Table 1.1: Summary of Test Findings

Test	Summary of Major Findings
Verbal Comprehension (WISCVC)	Score of 108 is high average showing marginally advanced verbal reasoning ability (e.g. thinking and expressing self with words). Tina's VC subtest scores ranged from 11/11 (classification of word pairs; oral definitions of words) to 13 (practical/social understanding). The subtest average is 10.
Perceptual Organisation (WISCPO)	Score of 96 is average, showing age-appropriate visual reasoning ability (e.g. thinking with pictures, analysing visual relationships). Tina's PO subtest score range was from 8/8 (reproducing models with three dimensional blocks; understanding pattern logic) to 12 (identifying themes across rows of pictures). The subtest average is 10.

(Continued)

Table 1.1: (*Continued*)

Test	Summary of Major Findings
Working Memory (WISCWR)	WM measures the ability to keep information in conscious awareness and perform an immediate operation with the information. Tina's score of 88 shows a level of working memory slightly below normal limits. Her subtest scores were 7 (immediate forward/backward recall and sequencing of numbers) and 9 (immediate recall of numbers/letters in a prescribed sequence).
Processing Speed (WISCPS)	PS involves the rapid and accurate scanning of visual symbols. The two PS tasks are paper and pencil speed tests. Tina's score of 103 is average. One of her subtest scores was 10 (copying shapes) while the other was 11 (discriminating between similar looking shapes).
Full Scale Score (WISCFULL)	The Full Scale Score is an estimate of overall cognitive ability. Tina's Full Scale Score of 100 (50th percentile)[*] shows general cognitive ability in the average band.
Word Reading (WIATWR)	This is a measure of word pronunciation skill. Tina's WIATWR standard score of 73 (4th percentile) is well below average. A sample of errors: 'de/pewt' for 'deputy', 'crutley' for 'cutlery' and 'showler' for 'scholar'.
Word Reading (WRATWR) (Blue)	This measure was administered as a second estimate of word reading level. Tina's WRATWR standard score was 80 (9th percentile).

(Continued)

Table 1.1: (*Continued*)

Test	Summary of Major Findings
Reading Comprehension (WIATRC)	The WIATRC task requires the student to read passages and answer oral questions about them. Tina obtained a WIATRC standard score of 102 (55th percentile), which is average and significantly higher than her two word reading scores. This reading pattern (comprehension being better than word reading accuracy) is elaborated on later in the report. Of five expository reading passages, all of her reading times were well above 90 words per minute (wpm) indicating a very fast reading speed. She correctly read 17 of 22 target words (23 per cent error rate).
Spelling (WIATSP)	WIATSP requires the student to write an orally presented word. Tina's WIATSP standard score of 78 (7th percentile) is well below average. As Tina miscued on start point words (e.g. 'ruff' for 'rough'), reverse administration was required to establish her skill level. Specifically, words designed for younger age groups were given to determine her baseline spelling level.
Spelling (WRATSP) (Blue)	This measure was administered to obtain a second estimate of word spelling skill. Tina's WRATSP standard score was 78 (7th percentile).
Written Expression (WIATWE)	Tina's essay component of this test is provided at the end of this report. Her WIATWE standard score was 94 with an associated percentile rank of 34.
Numerical Operations (WIATNO)	This is a computational test (e.g. 735 ÷ 15). Tina's WIATNO standard score of 101 (53rd percentile) is average. Students perform basic computations without the aid of a calculator.

* The percentile rank indicates the percentage of the comparison sample that perform to this level; if a percentile rank is 50, this means that 50 per cent of the comparison group perform at, or below, this standard.

Informal Measures

Behavioural Observations

Tina completed all tests in a focused and motivated manner. She was cheerful and possessed a sense of humour, often chuckling at her misspellings.

Parent/Client Report (summarised below)

Tina completed the standard Junior Certificate cycle. She sat the Junior Certificate exam in 2013 and was granted a spelling waiver for her language subjects, English, Irish and German.

She has just completed Transition Year. Her Leaving Certificate subjects will be English, Irish, German, Maths, Accounting, Home Economics, Biology and the LCVP module.

Summary and Comment

The reason for this assessment is determining Tina's cognitive profile. There are three general 'disability' categories this psychologist considers with respect to Tina's cognitive outcomes, which are detailed in Table 1.2, with the final row devoted to Tina's relative strengths.

Table 1.2: Summary of Tina's Cognitive Profile

Cognitive Profile	Comment
Specific learning disability (dyslexia) (ability high relative to low attainment)	Yes, very significant
General learning disability (ability and attainment low)	No
Comprehension disability (comprehension tests lower relative to non-comprehension tests)	No
Relative and/or normative strengths	WISC-IV verbal comprehension

Across various definitions of dyslexia, there are two main criteria for specific learning disability (SLD) (also known as dyslexia):

- *General cognitive ability in or above the 'average' band:* General cognitive ability is the WISC-IV Full Scale Score (or General Ability Index) and the 'average' band is a standard score between 90 and 110. Tina meets this criterion as her WISC-IV Full Scale Score is 100.
- *Attainment in literacy is 'below average':* The attainment tests are the WIAT-II/WRAT-4 word reading, reading comprehension, spelling and written expression measures. Tina meets this criterion as her word reading/spelling attainments are all 'well below average'.

A third criterion I typically observe is *uneven attainment*, namely:

- *WIAT-II reading comprehension is greater than WIAT-II/WRAT-4 word reading:* Note in the first criterion for a specific learning disability the assumption is a general cognitive ability score in, or above, the 'average' band. Therefore, dyslexic students are adept at reasoning, critical thinking and comprehension. It follows that a person skilled at reasoning will be able to grasp what is read, even when mis-pronouncing words in a passage. On the other hand, word analysis difficulty is the core symptom of SLD (dyslexia) and even the most intelligent dyslexic student can demonstrate unexpected delay in word recognition/pronunciation.
- *WIAT-II written expression is greater than WIAT-II/WRAT-4 word spelling:* The logic is similar to the previous point in that written expression includes more 'complex' thinking, such as organisation, theme development and vocabulary. Tina's writing sample (see below) is organised and reasonably well developed. On the other hand, her 'mechanics' score is extremely low (e.g. problems with spelling/grammar/punctuation).
- *WIAT-II numerical operations (maths) is greater than word reading/spelling attainments:* Tina's WIAT-II numerical operation

score of 101 is higher compared to her word reading and spelling attainments.

Summary of Cognitive Profile

Specific Learning Disability (Dyslexia)

- *Degree: Very significant* based on a large discrepancy between 'well below average' WIAT-II/WRAT-4 word reading and spelling attainments and 'average' general ability (WISC-IV Full Scale Score of 100).
- *Area(s) most impacted:* Word reading accuracy, spelling and aspects of written expression (i.e. mechanics).

Recommendations

1. Leaving Certificate Cycle Subjects

- Tina qualifies for the *National University of Ireland (NUI) exemption from the third language requirement.* As the enclosed form specifies, Tina can be admitted to any NUI college with one language (English). She can substitute another subject for the third language. The basis for her exemption is her severe and specific learning disability (dyslexia).
- Tina qualifies for *the NUI exemption from Irish.* Once again, as the certification form explains, Tina can present to any NUI campus with English as the only language subject for the same reason.
- The NUI exemption form was signed and provided at the completion of the assessment.

2. Reasonable Accommodation for Certificate Examination

Exam Reader

With regard to eligibility for an exam reader (a separate exam room with a designated individual to read exam material), the guidelines for psychologists in the 2013 Reasonable Accommodation for Certificate Examination (RACE) document require the following:

- *Indication of SLD for RACE*: Tina meets this criterion as noted in the preceding section of this report.
- *Standard scores of less than 85 on word reading tests*: Tina meets this criterion as her two word reading standard scores ranged from 73 to 80.
- *Evidence of difficulty reading connected text*, as manifest through (a) reading rates below 90 wpm or (b) reading accuracy error rate greater than 7 per cent. Tina meets (b), as her error rate on orally read material was 23 per cent (she incorrectly reading five of twenty-two target words on the WIAT-II reading comprehension oral reading samples).

As Tina meets all criteria, an exam reader is recommended.

Spelling Waiver

Using RACE Guidelines (2013), there are three qualifying criteria for a spelling waiver (spelling/grammar/punctuation will not be marked/penalised on language papers):

- *Indication of SLD*: Tina meets this criterion as noted in the preceding section.
- *Standard scores equal to or less than 85 on spelling tests*: Tina meets this criterion as both of her word spelling standard scores were below 85.
- *Spelling/grammar/punctuation error rate of 8 per cent or greater*: Tina's error rate is above this criterion as her SPG cumulative errors was 15 per cent of the total word count (see Tina's written sample, given at the end of the report).

Therefore, it is recommended that Tina be granted a waiver for spelling, grammar and punctuation/capitalisation for the English, Irish and German papers.

3. Third-Level Supports

Reasonable Accommodation for Course Examinations

- *Exam reader*: Rationale is provided in Recommendation 2
- *Spelling waiver*: Rationale is provided in Recommendation 2
- *Own room*

Assistive Technology

Not applicable.

Learning Support/Academic Tuition

Tina may require regular follow-up and assistance through the student support service at the third-level institution she attends. Support would involve reading, spelling and written expression.

Assignments/Laboratories

- *Proof reader*: A proof reader will be very important for long essays and final year projects (theses, dissertations, etc.). The proof reader is a designated staff member of the college Tina attends who will review her final papers to minimise problems associated with spelling, grammar, and punctuation.
- *Waiver for spelling* on essay assignments.

Lecture Supports

Not applicable.

4. Ideas and Handouts for Parents/Tina

- Tina meets the Disability Access Route to Education (DARE) criteria for a specific learning disability (dyslexia).
- Record (on any form of portable recording device) someone else reading the material to be learned. Tina can then repeatedly

listen to the oral rendition of the material until it is learned. The advantage is that oral input will relieve the dual strain of reading and memorising by changing the input format from visual to auditory. Auditory input will allow Tina to concentrate entirely on memorisation without the challenge of correct textual reading.

5. Cognitive Strengths and University Degree Course

- Using Tina's relative strengths as a guide to future third-level study, one area would be maths (WIAT-II numerical operations). Maths skills are essential to a variety of professions, such as engineering, business, accounting, economics and computer science.
- She is also skilled in verbal comprehension (oral language). Verbal ability can be linked to persuasive careers, such as sales, marketing, advertising, law and politics.

6. Review

Further assessment is not required.

William K. Wilkinson, EdD
Registered Psychologist, Psychological Society of Ireland

TINA'S WRITTEN EXPRESSION SAMPLE

A writing sample was obtained using the WIAT-II written expression format (prompt A: the writer argues for/against physical education in school). Tina's writing sample is provided below.

To whom it conurens,

I am wrighting this letter to you to state my opinion on P.E. I am for P.E and think it should be complurisy.

My reasons for saying this are simple Firstly as many Irish children are now over waight and suffer from helth promlems it is importent that they get some excirse at least once a week. Not only can it keep chilren from being over waight it can improve there health as it gets blood flowing to all parts of the body.

P.E also helps improve school work Studies have shown that children that excirse have better school work then thoes that just sit down and watch tv or use a computer.

My last reason for P.E is it help children get involed in out of school actives and betters friendships and they can meet people that they wouldnt have meet if they did not have to do some excirse once a week.

Your faithfully Tina

Comment

- Written words per minute = 16; a wpm score of 12 or greater is considered normal.
- Some words were difficult to read due to small block writing.
- A total of roughly 25 spelling/grammar/punctuation (SGP) errors. The overall SGP error rate is 15 per cent.
- The essay is well organised, including an introduction, separate paragraphs for supports and linking terms ('Firstly', 'last', etc.).
- There is back-up evidence regarding the second support (i.e. 'Studies have shown ...').

****

SUMMARY

The methods and outcomes in the example report were used to determine whether a previous problem – specific learning disability – is still significant and, if so, what recommendations are now relevant. During the initial conversation with the parent, the assessing psychologist can decide which methods are required to address the suspected problem.

The actual methods and outcomes used in evaluations will be discussed in the next two chapters. The methods are divided into two general categories: subjective and objective.

2

Assessment Methods – Subjective Sources

The information gathered in an assessment varies along a continuum from subjective to objective. Subjective sources are less structured compared to objective methods. For example, an unstructured interview with parents can take a number of forms, depending on the ebb and flow of dialogue. Parents might highlight a family matter, an incident at school, a question about health and its relationship to learning, what regimes work/do not work, previous assistance, and so on. Each topic requires attention by the assessing psychologist. The point is that the dialogue of an interview is somewhat unique to each case, given the unique personalities of those involved.

Subjective materials also tend to be less quantitative and numerical relative to objective methods. For example, when reading previous reports, the assessing psychologist usually gleans an overall impression from the previous diagnostician. There is no attempt to quantify the report. Or, when observing an individual solving problems, the psychologist may note how they approach the task. For example, if asked to repeat a set of numbers in backward sequence, do they repeat the series in the forward direction before attempting to reverse the number string? How do they cope with items which become increasingly challenging as a particular test progresses? Again, this is a narrative, descriptive approach, one which does not provide numbers or statistics.

By way of contrast, the objective approach is more structured and numerical. There is a strong element of repetition of procedural sequence, that is, the same materials are presented in the same way to each new participant. And, at the end of the process, there is a number, with a particular meaning. The number of correct answers, known as a raw score, is then converted a standard score. The standard score is obtained from conversion tables in the technical manual that accompanies the particular test. As the name implies, the standard score enables the psychologist to compare the ability of the person being tested to that of other children of similar age.

Both subjective and objective approaches are vital in an assessment. While numbers are important, so are the myriad ways in which people interact with materials. Do they give up easily? Do they persist? What about concentration as the test sequence continues past the two-hour mark? How do they express emotions?

Likewise, it would be foolish not to incorporate the parents' perspectives. What are the long-standing issues which emerge from the parents' observations? An assessment is a structured meeting with the child and sometimes the ingrained patterns which are often observed at home are not apparent in the assessment process. For example, parents may find that their child is inattentive and unable to concentrate for any significant period of time while doing mental work (e.g. school work) at home. Yet, under assessment conditions, the same child might be able to persist and concentrate for the two-and-a-half-hour testing period. No problems with attention span are noted in the assessment, yet parents report significant issues with concentration at home. A discussion with the parents will help to identify the reasons for the differing attention spans.

Introducing the Assessment

The appointment starts with an introductory meeting designed to put parents and children at ease. For primary school children, after everyone is seated, the psychologist may direct several questions to the child: What is the name of your school? What class are you in? Do you get any extra help in school for reading or maths? Some children communicate easily and freely, providing details; others are quiet and less talkative. As the first few moments are designed to put people at ease, this group meeting is very informal, and very much conversational rather than in a formal interview style.

Subsequently, the psychologist will introduce the activities to you and your child. They explain what your child will do, the kinds of tasks involved (reading, maths, visual games, etc.) and usually show samples of some of the materials. Again, this is to familiarise everyone with the actual methods. In this conversation, it is important that the psychologist explains that some items are for younger children and will be easy while others are for older children and may be challenging. Another equally important message is to 'do your best and don't worry if you don't know all the answers.'

At this point, an important juncture occurs, which is the separation process. For younger children, parents may wait in an adjoining waiting room. In my office, for example, a door connects the office and waiting area. Everything is audible and there can be partial visual contact if the door is ajar. If the child or parents do not want to separate, then a parent can stay in the office while the testing sequence occurs. However, a parent remaining in the office is not advisable, and not very common, as the dynamic between child and psychologist is altered. Many times, the child will look to the parent for assistance. If you do remain in the office, the key is to be invisible and not interact, visually or verbally, with your child. For older students (e.g. later primary and secondary school age), parents usually do not stay and return to the office after a two-and-a-half-to-three-hour interval.

Once the separation process concludes, the formal assessment begins. During the time with the child, two subjective sources of information are gathered: the child interview and behaviour observations. These are discussed next.

CHILD INTERVIEW

The timing, process and content of dialogue with the child depends greatly on age. For younger children, familiarity is important so the psychologist will begin with the tasks most similar to school (e.g. reading, maths). Once standardised testing commences, the verbal interchange with younger children may be minimal. In fact, the idea of a formal 'interview' does not occur. Why?

First, attention span and mental stamina are required to complete roughly two hours of standardised tests. A dedicated interview would reduce the mental focus needed simply to complete all the tests in a given period. The more time is allocated for an interview, the less time there is to complete a standardised test sequence.

Second, much of the dialogue with younger children happens naturally during the testing. Children may comment on a test item, or mention some aspect of schooling or home life. These comments are the springboard for further discussion and the basis for informal conversation. When spontaneous conversation occurs, the child is comfortable in the assessment context and demonstrates interpersonal skills. There is no expectation that any exchange will be greatly revealing. However, sometimes, a child might make an interesting comment (e.g. 'Are you going to tell me what is wrong with me?'). If this happens, the psychologist will likely note what was said and share it with the parents.

For older children, particularly those in secondary school, the interview may take a more formal structure. For example, the psychologist may use a form or checklist which covers a broad range of topics – family, school, recreational activities, likes/dislikes, etc. The information might be collected before the psychologist starts standardised testing as a means to establish rapport. Or, if the psychologist does not use a recording form, information is communicated spontaneously during standardised testing. For example, students often comment on test materials, which creates an opportunity for discussion. If the student finds a particular test challenging, the psychologist can ask how the problem relates to school and homework. Conversely, if a clear skill is manifest this can lead to informal conversation about how the specific strength translates to specific areas of the curriculum, recreational activities and potential career interests.

Again with older students, the psychologist might use a self-reported standardised rating scale (rating scales will be discussed in more detail in Chapter 3). In the context of these ratings, the psychologist can pursue the student's responses in a variety of areas, such as social connection, academic skills, hobbies, concentration, organisation, study habits, memory and attitude. In this case, important communication is embedded in a standardised rating instrument.

For adults, there is a more structured and detailed background interview covering employment and education history, family and relationships, nature of the problem, interventions to date, and so on. This interview occurs before standardised testing and can last up to 90 minutes.

It is necessary to distinguish the type of communication that occurs during an educational assessment from what happens during a child counselling/psychotherapy session. The information shared by a student during educational assessment is anecdotal and indirect. The assessing psychologist is not focusing on dialogue and long conversations with the child; instead, the emphasis is on ensuring that the child cooperates and concentrates throughout so that the obtained test results are valid. On the other hand, if the child is attending a psychologist for therapy then the focus is entirely on communication, talking and dialogue. As there will be repeated and briefer sessions, the psychologist will focus on the child's perception of the problem – what they think, how they feel, what they do, etc. The psychologist will have a particular theoretical view (e.g. cognitive behavioural therapy) which is used to structure the communication and lead the child to insight and, ultimately, positive behaviour change. During these first therapeutic meetings, the psychologist may use a structured (or semi-structured) interview covering a number of topics – family, school, friends, interests, feelings, health, etc. Standardised testing will not be a factor at the initial stages of therapy, although it might be recommended at a later date.

Even though the dialogue is brief during an assessment, it is sometimes the case that children's comments provide insights into their self-esteem and their perception of the problem. This information can have direct bearing on the recommendations made by the psychologist. For example, students who struggle with written expression may report difficulty organising their ideas into a coherent and well-structured essay. This comment can help the psychologist develop specific recommendations to improve the organisational element of writing (e.g. mind-mapping techniques). Assessing psychologists may find associations between a child's comments and information derived from other sources. For example, children who enjoy drawing or playing with Lego often display well-developed visual reasoning ability. Or, if a child is very active during an assessment and informs the psychologist that they find it hard to stay seated in class, this comment will fit with other perceptions and assist the psychologist in formulating a diagnostic conclusion.

BEHAVIOUR OBSERVATIONS

Very much intermingled with the child interview, behaviour observations are an integral part of an assessment. Read any psychologist's report and there will be a section referring to 'behaviour during the assessment'. Where do these observations occur? How does one observe behaviour? Are observations of behaviour useful?

Obviously, psychologists observe behaviour in the environment of the assessment. Some psychologists have dedicated offices for assessment, and the child is observed in the office/clinic. Others may test in the child's home and thus observations occur in this context. Or, if the psychologist travels to the school, observations occur at school (in the classroom or school yard) and during structured testing. In situations where behaviour and social functioning are reasons for referral, there is an obvious advantage to observing the child in school. Unfortunately, this is not always possible for practical reasons, namely cost and time.

How does one observe behaviour? A psychologist will observe and record behaviour throughout the session. If the child makes a comment, this might be noted; if their speech is difficult to understand, this will be recorded; if the child refuses to cooperate, this will certainly be a focus of the written report. Indeed, the most essential observation is whether the child meaningfully engages with test materials. In other words, does the psychologist feel that the results of the tests administered accurately reflect the child's true skill levels? Or, does the child not cooperate so that the formal testing procedure cannot be administered, or can only be partially administered.

Take for example, the following case (with identifying details altered):

John (aged ten) refused to enter the office, sitting in a chair in the adjoining waiting room while his parents met the psychologist. After several minutes, he left the room by the front door. His father brought him back to the office and the front door was locked. At this point, he banged on the door and repeatedly turned the door handle (when the assessment was concluded, it was noted that the door handle was loosened by the force of his continually turning and banging it; likewise, flecks of paint were found at the bottom of the door).

At the psychologist's request, John's mother 'physically prompted' him to sit in the office. While she held him, he repeatedly kicked and hit her. A task in which the child constructs a pictured model with three-dimensional blocks was introduced. John knocked all the blocks off the desk. He then left the chair, and tried to leave the office. Again, he kept turning the handle and whining. This was ignored and he eventually asked to watch television. The psychologist asked John if he wish to watch a video but, after looking at the videos on offer, he did not wish to watch any of them.

After a long period of cajoling (roughly 45 minutes after the family arrived), John engaged in an activity of his choice (drawing). He completed the first three items on the block design test before saying 'I'm not doing anymore.' He did the same on another picture-oriented test where he was asked to find the theme across rows of pictures. He completed the first ten items and then refused to do any more.

When introduced to tasks he did not select (e.g. paper and pencil speed tests), he would do the first few items correctly, then randomly make marks in each shape. On a verbal test, he gave the correct response to the sample item then gave random and incorrect responses to the remaining questions (e.g. repeating one of the words in the question). Before he left the office to return to the waiting room, he asked for a paper clip so he could try to unlock the door. Soon thereafter, he entered the bathroom and climbed out a small window. He then remained outside with his father.

In this case, the core testing sequence could not be administered and the behaviour observations were of paramount importance. John's defiance and non-compliance indicate an obvious problem, although this would need to be verified across settings and people.

In the second case, all tests were administered to a fourteen-year-old girl. There were many revealing interactions during the assessment.

During the first half of the assessment, Missy related in a confrontational manner. For example, after completing a word reading list, she said the list was too hard. She asked if she could read the list again. On the next test, she looked at the passage and said she had just done that test two or three weeks previously. At this point, she said she was not going to do the tests again and could I call her parents. To complete the assessment, a decision was made to use different tests.

Subsequently, she completed a measure of reading comprehension, continually asking how many more she had to do. She noticed markings on a score sheet and asked, 'Are those all wrong?'

On the spelling test, she again asked how she did, what was above/below average, what was the highest score possible, and so on. When asked to provide a writing sample, she asked why she had to complete a writing test. She cooperated, but only wrote for three minutes (of a fifteen-minute time allotment). She completed the maths test quickly and without comment (other than to ask if she could use a calculator).

When we started ability testing, Missy again recognised test items and pouted about doing the tasks again. However, given her intense interest in her performance, she was informed that she would be given feedback after each test. This had the effect of piquing her interest and she was very easy to relate to for the remainder of the assessment. At these times, she conversed in an open fashion and several spontaneous conversations developed (for example, she asked whether I knew certain professionals she met in the past several months).

In the above example, all tests were completed, but the conditions of interaction were unusual. For example, immediate feedback was provided in order to maintain Missy's motivation. In the absence of this contingency, Missy would not have cooperated and the assessment would be limited in scope.

In the above examples, behaviour interfered with the normal assessment procedure. In some cases, the tests used are beyond the grasp of the child, even at the simplest and youngest age levels. Take the following case:

Initially, Peter, age six, willingly entered the office with his mother. He had a DVD and a roll of Sellotape in his hands. He continually peeled off pieces of Sellotape and had a number of tape pieces stuck to the DVD cover. He also tried to place a small bit of tape on his face. He continually played with the Sellotape for the duration of the assessment.

During an initial conversation with Peter's mother, he occasionally interjected with a comment but did not answer questions directed to him. Usually, he looked at his mother or repeated a word he recognised. He often screamed a word or a two-or-three-word sentence. He was asked by his mother to stop screaming, but this request had little effect.

We commenced standardised testing. It was obvious that the test items were not at an appropriate developmental level for Peter. For example, he was asked to find the missing piece of a picture. For the youngest age groups, the first pictures indicate an extremely conspicuous missing piece, for example an ear is omitted from an animal. However, Peter did not understand the task, as words like 'missing' were incomprehensible to him. While he could name the picture, the idea of identifying what was missing was not in his repertoire. He was also inattentive at this time, scanning the room but not making eye contact with the test materials or the psychologist. He was repeatedly asked to 'look', which was not effective.

A similar mis-match was noted for the majority of the remaining tests, where Peter did not obtain a raw score. On two tests, he responded to one item (e.g. counting three birds). He could not count beyond three. He obtained partial credit for 'ding-dong' in response to the question, 'What is a clock?' He was able to connect a few puzzle pieces on several puzzles. He did not respond to the simplest words on the reading list. He was asked to write letters of the alphabet but took the pencil and scribbled. After talking with Peter's mother, it was decided not to attempt sums (e.g. 3 + 3), as Peter is not familiar with maths.

Further non-standardised testing was attempted to get a rough idea of exactly what Peter could and could not do. He was asked to name the object which briefly appeared in a small slit on a cardboard disk. Peter was intrigued with this test and focused well on the task. He named half the objects. He was then requested to identify a series of partially completed drawings. Peter named four items. Subsequently, he could name fourteen common objects (e.g. window, banana, mug, scissors and ear). Finally, when asked to copy simple geometric shapes (e.g. |, —), he took the pencil and scribbled.

During the parent meeting, Peter waited in an adjoining waiting room. He watched DVDs and was typically settled. There were several moments when he was upset (e.g. screaming) but this abated quickly and he returned to his viewing. On two occasions, he asked to use the bathroom and his mother assisted him at these times. He infrequently made a comment like 'We going now?'

In this case, Peter was unable to engage with the tests because he did not have the mental ability to do so. When this occurs, the objective is to determine the skills in the child's repertoire so that further teaching could progress from the starting levels identified.

All of the above examples are known as 'narrative' recording. The goal is to provide a detailed and rich description of events. The narrative method is the most common method in time-limited assessments. Typically, the psychologist will have a number of categories in mind while observing, such as physical appearance (which, personally, I feel is the least relevant, except in rare cases), speech and language, unusual mannerisms, interpersonal skills (does the child engage in casual conversation, eye contact, etc.), mood, attention span and self-concept, to name a few.

In the vast majority of cases, the behaviour observations are brief and positive. In some cases, any difficult or unusual behaviour will be stated in the report (as illustrated in the previous examples). When the behaviour observation section is brief, the reader of the report would be safe in assuming that the person was generally easy to assess and there were no major issues worth reporting (e.g. behaviour/emotional issues, or unusual or eccentric habits). An example of the majority of observations would be summarised by the following:

> Barbara was an ideal student to assess. She undertook all tests in a cooperative and positive attitude and was persistent as problems increased in difficulty.

PREVIOUS REPORTS

In some cases, a child may have been previously assessed by a professional in the disciplines of speech and language therapy, occupational therapy, psychiatry or psychology. If available, these reports should be provided to the assessing psychologist. Other potential reports include school report cards, teacher narrative reports, even samples of a child's work (child work samples are not reports per se, but represent information available to a psychologist). There are also standard referral forms which summarise information pre-assessment and can be made available to the assessing psychologist. An example school referral form is provided below:

****

SCHOOL REFERRAL FORM

Name of child: _____ Date of birth: _____
Parent/guardian names: _____
Address: _____
Telephone number – Home: _____ Work: _____
School address: _____
School phone number: _____ Class teacher: _____
Class: _____

Main Reason for Referral (mark those that apply):

Learning: _____ Behavioural: _____
Emotional: _____ Other: _____
Elaborate: _____
Classes repeated: _____
_____
Does the child receive learning support? If yes, please give details (number in group, how many times per week, how long is each support session): _____
_____

What types of interventions have been used (please be specific): ___
_____
School tests administered (list name and result): _____
_____
_____

Please comment on the following areas:

- Listening skill: _____
- Memory: _____
- Concentration/attention span: _____
- Oral language: _____
- Reading: _____
- Handwriting: _____
- Spelling: _____
- Numbers: _____
- Motor development: _____
- Relationship with adults: _____
- Relationship with peers: _____
- Behaviour in class: _____
- Behaviour in playground: _____

Additional comments (Please add any additional information you feel is relevant):

_____

_____

_____

_____

****

Psychologists usually summarise key elements of previous documents in their final report, either as part of the Background Information section or in a separately headed section (e.g. Review of Reports).

Occasionally, an issue arises as to whether previous reports should be provided to the assessing psychologist before the evaluation. Parents might feel that the information can somehow bias the assessment process. My view is that pre-referral information is very important in guiding what to assess. Again, there are a number of instruments and methods available and only so much time to assess the child. In the absence of any pre-referral information, there is a risk that the psychologist might engage in a general assessment and miss the opportunity to focus on the particular issue that is of concern. Obviously, one would hope that the parents and/or teachers would communicate the nature of their concern during the initial conversation, or at least during the parent meeting. If the results of the preliminary assessment do not illuminate any significant issue, further assessment could be conducted based on what parents report (specific instruments could be completed by parents during this time).

Each child is a blank slate, regardless of what information is received before the appointment. The testing process is so standardised and methodical that there is little room for bias. Again, the main purpose of the standardised testing sequence is to ensure that all data is collected and that the results truly reflect what the child can do. If difficult or non-optimal test behaviour occurs, this will be noted and checked against behaviour at home/school.

Parent Interview

While psychologists may differ in the order in which information is collected, my preference is to meet parents after the child assessment is completed. The main advantage of this sequence is, after introductions, the child settles into what appears to be a school-type routine.

After the child is assessed, there is a threefold purpose to the parent interview. Obviously, one is to gather vital information from parents about the nature of their concerns. The second is providing feedback about the results of standardised tests and behaviour observations. The third is to recommend a plan to address the concerns that emerge from assessment and the parent meeting.

While the third element will inevitably be the last item on the agenda, the first two are interwoven. For example, if parents ask a direct question, such as 'What did you find?', I provide a direct answer. Since standardised test results are in graph form on my desktop, it is easy to refer to this chart to explain the outcomes. On the rare occasion that a child's behaviour was challenging (as in the examples above), then the behaviour issues observed during the assessment become the springboard for discussion. If parents do not start the meeting with a question and behaviour was without issue (which it normally is), I might ask parents 'Why have you decided to have your son/daughter assessed?'

The interweaving of interview and feedback is less structured than a formal list of questions to parents, which could occur at the outset of the parent meeting. I prefer the give-and-take method as it puts everyone on an equal footing. After all, parents know more about their children than anyone else; their knowledge and insights are essential to the process. I feel my job is to create a safe, mutual exchange environment which enables parents to say whatever they feel is relevant. The mutual sharing of collective knowledge and insights is the best way to encourage honesty and collaborative problem solving.

The parent interview process occurs whether one or two parents attend. Obviously, it is not always possible for both parents to meet the psychologist, especially given other children, work schedules, travel, etc. However, the ideal is for both parents to attend as each parent will have an individual take as well as a common perception of the assessed child. Different attitudes and valuable information may emerge during the meeting, such as one parent being around the child more than the other or one parent being stricter than the other. There is nothing unusual about differing perceptions and parenting styles, and communicating these to the interviewing psychologist can be important for parents.

On rare occasions, I find that one parent may be disengaged during the meeting, usually the father. This can happen for several reasons. One is that the father may have less involvement in and knowledge about his child's education relative to the mother. Sometimes, in the division of labour, it is the mother who attends parent–teacher meetings and school functions. Hence the mother may be the source of information regarding all things educational.

Also, and again rare as it is, parents may not believe in the need for an assessment, which they might demonstrate by remaining silent for the entire meeting, by looking like they would rather be anywhere but in the psychologist's office. When this happens my strategy is to try to involve the 'quiet parent'. If this fails, I might point out that it is my guess that they do not believe in the need for an assessment. If the silent parent concurs, this can start a dialogue.

For some parents, the types of verbal interaction skills required to usefully engage with the psychologist are not well developed. For example, some parents may have difficulty describing or elaborating on the issues of concern to them. In other cases, English might not be the first language of the family. Certainly for some parents, the thought of a lengthy interview with a stranger about their child can be off-putting. This is another reason why I prefer the give-and-take method: the idea of a formal interview is immediately dispelled. If the psychologist is a parent, or if they have attended an assessment for one of their own children, these experiences increase understanding and empathy, and may allow for a more frank and candid exchange.

As a general guideline, the following suggestions are provided to parents before meeting the psychologist. First, there must be a pressing concern that led to the appointment. Therefore, you should not to minimise the problem, or couch it in a number of 'it depends'. You must be emphatic as to the nature and extent of the problem. For example, if your child's activity level is absurdly high, do not make a statement like 'Well, all children are active.' Again, why is your child being assessed? Clearly, they are there because of some learning/behavioural/social/motor problem. You should never underestimate the fact that a referral for an assessment assumes a significant concern.

Of course, what if the referral is school based, with the parents attending at the school's request? In this situation, parents may not perceive the problem or may have a different take on the school situation. Differences in school and parental perception are understandable. Obviously, learning, social and behaviour elements are highlighted for an entire school day, whereas at home the environment is more about down-time and play. Clearly, behaviour differences will emerge given the unique and differing expectations of home and school. The goal of the psychologist is to understand and explain to parents how a child's behaviour may differ at home and school. Sometimes, one can use differences in the child's behaviour between situations to construct interventions. For example, what if a child has difficulty concentrating at home, but not at school? In this situation, the psychologist can provide parents with a plan to increase academic productivity at home (these methods are discussed in Chapter 6).

The second consideration is whether parents disclose all relevant information. Obviously, it is up to parents to decide what is relevant. Sometimes, there may be family or personal issues that parents consciously avoid mentioning. For example, there may be an element of marital discord. Do parents need to report this issue if their child displays a particular problem with spelling/writing? Probably not. On the other hand, if the reason for referral is a behavioural or emotional problem, then information about family relationship patterns is valuable. I have enough respect for parents (and parenting) to acknowledge that whatever information is disclosed or not disclosed, it is ultimately the parents' choice.

If psychologists do engage parents using a structured format, a standard parent questionnaire may look something like this:

****

BACKGROUND INFORMATION – FOR PARENTS

Name of child: _____ Date of birth: _____
Parent/guardian names: _____
Address: _____
Telephone number – Home: _____ Work: _____
Today's date: _____
Name of person completing this form: _____
Relationship to child: _____
Name of school: _____ Class in school: _____

Family
List all people living in house:

Name	Relationship to Child	Age
_____	_____	____
_____	_____	____
_____	_____	____
_____	_____	____

Names and ages of brothers/sisters not living at home: _____

Primary language at home: _____

Primary Concern (please describe your child's current difficulties): __

_____

_____

When did you first notice the problem? _____

_____

What strategies have you used to deal with the problem? Do these strategies work or help, or do efforts to help make the problem worse? _____

_____

_____

Please comment on your child in the following areas:

- Behaviour: _____
- Relationship with other family members: _____

_____

- Relationship with peers: _____

_____

- Learning (does your child have any difficulties at school with reading, writing or maths?): _____

_____

- Development (any concerns/delays in walking, talking, toilet training): _____
- Independent living skills (dressing, eating, hygiene, cleaning up):
- Medical/health: Any chronic conditions? Any significant illnesses or injuries? Current health, including hearing/vision:

_____

- What are your child's interests/favourite activities? _____

_____

****

By the time the meeting has concluded, the psychologist will likely have covered the following areas of development:

1. *Social*: Does your child have friends? Do they interact with same age peers? Do they demonstrate social–emotional skills: empathy, give and take in conversation, etc.
2. *Behaviour*: Does your child have any problems with challenging or difficult behaviour – arguing, tantrums, anger, excess activity, inability to concentrate/study, etc. Do they have any unusual behaviour or routines (e.g. odd movements/gestures, strange play habits)? Again, while all children might engage in some of this behaviour some of the time, the key is whether the problem is significantly impairing your child's learning and relationships with others.
3. *Emotional*: What is your child's prevailing mood? Are they anxious? Do they have any major fears or do they display avoidance-type behaviour?
4. *Motor and independent living skills*: Does your child dress him/herself? Do they have any problems with coordination, such as buttons/shoelaces? Are they involved in sport? How are their handwriting skills – is it legible, is it slow and laboured, or do they have an unusual pencil grip?
5. *Health*: Does your child have any chronic illnesses or significant injuries? Do they have any problems with their hearing and sight? What are their diet and sleep patterns like?
6. *Interests*: How does your child spend their free time?

Ideally, all of these areas will be briefly covered and any significant details will be re-stated in the final report.

School and Home Visit

A school visit may be part of the assessment, particularly if the assessing psychologist is employed through the National Educational Psychological Service (NEPS). Psychologists working in the NEPS routinely engage in a school visit as part of the assessment. On the other hand, a private practice psychologist, like myself, is less likely to conduct a school visit due to issues of time and cost.

Of all the data collection methods, a school or home visit is the most optional. This is because a thorough school report will indicate and describe the nature of the problem at school. A school visit will simply serve to confirm the problem. The advantage of a school visit is the possibility of further insight into the extent of the problem and how to intervene.

Many referral problems do not require a school or home visit. For example, queries about specific learning disabilities are a common reason parents seek an assessment. A psychologist does not need to visit the home or school to detect a specific learning disability. This diagnosis is based entirely on standardised testing as conducted in a clinic/office.

Finally, with the widespread use and availability of recording equipment, some parents might capture a problem behaviour at home using a portable recording device. For example, low frequency but high intensity behaviour, such as rages/tantrums, can easily be recorded on a mobile phone. This information is useful in detailing the topography of behaviour – exactly what the child does when a tantrum occurs. However, the events leading up to the episode may not be easily recorded, as the entire behaviour sequence may take longer to develop than can be recorded using a time-limited device.

For a psychologist, there are many technical aspects to the science of recording behaviour during a home or school visit. Some basic questions are when and how the recording will occur. There are numerous forms available for recording, as well as methods to determine the accuracy of a home/school observation (e.g. cross-checking observations with another observing professional). Below is an example of an observational form.

A-B-C HOME/VISIT OBSERVATION FORM

Name of child: Michael
Date of birth: 25/12/2006
Time of observation: 2.45 p.m., Tuesday
Place of observation: Home
Activity/setting: Michael playing with toys in playroom

Directions:
Use this form to observe and record behaviour. An antecedent is what is happening (e.g. playing with Lego in a playroom, engaging in independent work in the classroom). Behaviour is the actions of the child in the context of the observation (e.g. making noise when playing with Lego, looking out the window when others in class are doing maths). A consequence is what happens when the child's behaviour occurs, such as the parent telling the child to play quietly and the child playing quietly and appropriately, or the teacher reminding the child to return to their maths work.

Antecedent	Behaviour	Consequence
1. Michael is playing with Lego in the playroom.	Michael is making loud noises and sound effects; he is playing roughly – crashing tower blocks of Lego onto the floor, against furniture, etc.	Parent says, 'Michael, play quietly' from another room. *Response to consequence*: Michael ignores his parent and continues to play as before.
2. Lego play	Michael continues his loud and rough play.	Parent enters room and directly tells Michael to play quietly. *Response to consequence*: Michael lowers the intensity and loudness of his play.

(Continued)

(*Continued*)		
Antecedent	**Behaviour**	**Consequence**
3. Lego play	Michael plays quietly and appropriately with Lego for five minutes.	No parent consequence.
4. Lego play	After five minutes of quiet and appropriate play, Michael resumes loud sound effects, including throwing blocks and banging blocks off furniture.	Parent enters room and takes Lego from Michael, noting that he did not listen to repeated requests to play quietly and appropriately. *Response to consequence*: Michael argues and says he will play quietly now. Parent agrees to allow Michael to play if he does so quietly.
5. Lego play	Michael ceases loud and aggressive play. Instead, he starts to build a farm area as illustrated in a picture.	No parent consequence.

What does one learn from this particular observation? Is it inappropriate for a child to play with Lego the way Michael did? Was there anything the parent could have done differently? Loud and boisterous play isn't necessarily a problem, unless it interferes with the concentration of others or damages toys or furnishings. Obviously, the parent's request for Michael to play more quietly was based on the general noise created and how loud sound effects create difficulty for others trying to concentrate (parent potentially speaking on phone, other children doing homework, etc.). The sequence of the parent's consequences would be common for many parents. Usually, there is a rise in voice before a more immediate consequence is forthcoming (e.g. removing the toys). On two occasions, the parent missed an opportunity to provide praise for quiet and appropriate toy play. If parental praise (or positive parental attention) for good behaviour results in the child behaving well in the future (in other words, parental praise is a positive reinforcer), then the parent could have increased the chance for more appropriate play in the future.

SUMMARY

We have discussed four essential subjective sources of information: the child interview, behaviour observations, reports/documents completed before the assessment, and the parent interview (the fifth source, home/school visit, is optional). In some cases, these sections will be combined in the final report. For example, the child interview may be part of the behaviour observations. Also, there are often no previous reports or documents that need to be summarised, so this section may not be in the final assessment report.

Subjective sources are important and can play a significant role in the final conclusion. For example, the behaviour observation examples lead one to make diagnostic references in the absence of any other data. In the first example, John's behaviour was extremely oppositional and defiant – he refused to engage in any task, was aggressive to his parents and the test materials, and made repeated attempts to escape. In the third example, Peter was unable to interact with the test materials, which indicates the significance of his learning-related difficulty. Also, some of his behaviour was very unusual, suggesting other underlying disabilities.

The parent interview is equally invaluable. If parents can clearly articulate their major concerns then the diagnostic process is greatly enhanced. It may be useful for parents to contemplate the nature of the problem and write down their main concerns before an appointment.

This written information can be provided to the psychologist or used to aid the discussion when the parents outline the key issues.

The next set of procedures is objective in nature and will be discussed in the following chapter.

3

Assessment Methods – Objective Sources

All objective sources have three main components: (a) standardisation, (b) norm-referenced and (c) numerical outcomes. Standardisation means that all measures are administered and scored in the same fashion. The measure, such as a rating scale or test, is administered to a sample in order to develop baseline standards by which each subsequent individual is referenced against. These standards, or 'norms', tell us how a person compares with a similar age group in regard to what the rating scale or test is measuring. The process of comparison results in a numerical outcome, which can go by any number of names: scale score, sten, percentile, reading age, etc. Many parents are familiar with frequently used school tests, such as Drumcondra, MICRA-T and SIGMA-T. In these tests your child may have received, say, a sten score of 3, a standard score of 87 or a percentile of 19. Since we have a numerical outcome on a standardised and norm-referenced measure, the source is considered objective.

There are a vast number of objective measures available to psychologists. In the context of psychoeducational assessments, there are a core set of measures that are commonly accepted and widely used. The widespread use of a particular measure implies that it meets the highest professional standards in terms of development, statistical properties and usefulness.

There are two broad categories of objective measures: rating scales and performance tests. Rating scales are generally completed by the parent and/or teacher. In addition, there are scales for children/

teenagers to complete. Rating scales consist of descriptive statements that are assigned a numerical value. The end result is a set of quantitative outcomes on the domains measured by the particular rating scale – memory, organisation, hyperactivity, anxiety, eccentric behaviour, independent living skills, etc.

People may be familiar with rating scales from completing surveys on the internet. These surveys use the same format as rating scales, but lack the scientific research and technical properties which define the instruments used in an assessment.

In contrast to rating scales, performance tests are tasks given to an individual to determine his/her skill levels. Skills may include verbal ability, memory, speed, reading and maths. The person's performance is then compared with those of a similar age group. The result is a numerical score which shows the person's standing relative to their age group.

In an assessment, the main purpose of rating scales relates to behavioural, emotional, social, motor and other development disabilities. On the other hand, performance tests are required to diagnose any suspected learning-related disability.

There are many types of rating scales and performance tests. The ones covered in this chapter are commonly used by many psychologists. However, you should be aware that there are different forms/versions of any one test, as well as numerous other methods which will not be covered here.

RATING SCALES

So how does a psychologist decide what rating forms to use? The choice of rating instruments depends on the concerns identified by the parent or teacher when referring the child for assessment. In the emotional, behavioural and social domains, the most common problems are attention deficit/hyperactivity disorder (AD/HD), oppositional defiant disorder (ODD) and Asperger syndrome (AS). There is a wide choice of rating scales for these types of issues. Most rating scales are completed by parents and teachers, such as the Conners' Scales and the Gilliam Asperger's Disorder Scale (GADS). The Conners' Scales is used to identify common behaviour problems, namely AD/HD and ODD. The GADS assists in determining the presence of an autistic spectrum disorder, specifically Asperger syndrome.

Some instruments include forms for children and adolescents to complete. For example, children and adolescents can complete self-report measures specific to AD/HD, such as the Brown Attention Deficit Disorder Scales.

If there is a concern about intellectual disability (ID) the assessing psychologist will use a measure of adaptive behaviour. One rating form often used is the Adaptive Behaviour Assessment System, second edition (ABAS-II).

Finally, career interests can be measured. As one example, the Rothwell–Miller Interest Blank (RMIB) will be covered.

Conners' Rating Scales

The instrument described here is an older, short-form version of the Conners' Rating Scales (a more comprehensive and updated rating form, also published by Conners, will be described in Chapter 4). The Conners' Rating Scale measures parent and teacher observations related to AD/HD and ODD. Teacher perceptions of a student's academic skills are also covered. The Conners' Rating Scale consists of two different ratings, one for parents and one for teachers. It is common for both forms to be completed so that the child's behaviour is reported in both home and school environments.

The rating form consists of 27 (parent version) or 28 (teacher version) statements. Examples of statements common to both forms are 'short attention span', 'argues with adults' and 'is always on the go or acts as if driven by a motor'. The person completing the form responds to each statement using a numerical index: 0 = not true at all; 1 = just a little true; 2 = pretty much true; 3 = very much true. Each item is part of a scale, which in the case of the Conners' Rating Scale – Revised (Short) are Oppositional, Cognitive Problems/Inattention, Hyperactivity/Impulsivity, and AD/HD Risk (four scales in total). The total item score for each scale is converted to a new number, which expresses how the person being rated is perceived relative to their age group. In the case of the Conners' Rating Scale, the new number is called a T-score. In the Conners manual, the T-score range is 38 to 90. The average T-score is 50 and T-scores greater than 65 indicate that the raters perceive a statistically significant level of the particular issue being measured. For example, consider the rating outcomes in Figure 3.1 for 'Aoife'.

Figure 3.1: Example Rating Outcomes for Short-Form Conners' Rating Scale

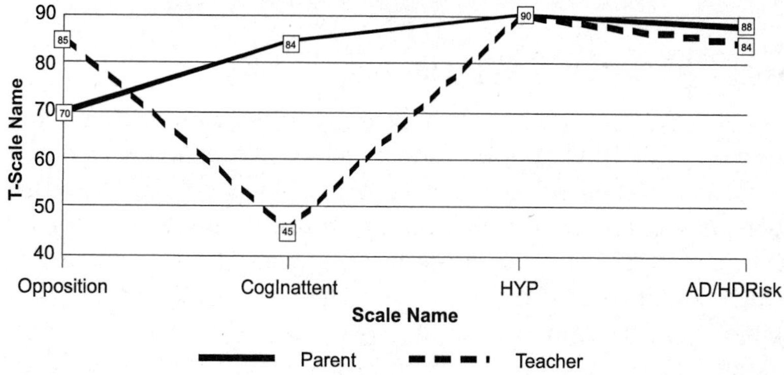

Starting with the left-hand label 'Opposition' and moving across, we can make the following interpretations:

- *Oppositional Behaviour (Opposition)* – This domain includes being likely to break rules, having trouble with authority, and being easily annoyed and angered. In this domain, Aoife is argumentative and non-compliant at home and school.
- *Cognitive Problems/Inattention (CogInattent)* – This scale measures different attributes depending on the rater. On the parent form, 'inattention' is highlighted, such as the type of sustained concentration required to complete homework. Aoife is perceived to be very distracted and inattentive in the home environment. On the other hand, on the teacher form, 'cognitive problems' are highlighted (e.g. basic academic skill deficits in reading, spelling and maths). The teacher found that Aoife's spelling, reading and maths skills are without issue.

- *Hyperactivity (HYP)* – As the name implies, this scale refers to excessive activity, such as being always on the go, having difficulty sitting still, and being more impulsive and restless than most children of their age. Aoife is observed to be extremely over-active and impulsive at home and school.
- *AD/HD Risk (AD/HDRisk)* – This is the most important domain as it contains relatively more items than the other scales and identifies those at risk of AD/HD. Both parents and teacher observe a 'very significant' degree of AD/HD type behaviour.

Brown Attention Deficit Disorder Scale

A rating scale for completion by students is the Brown Attention Deficit Disorder Scale (BADDS). In terms of self-reporting, the scale can be completed by children aged from eight to eighteen. Regardless of age, the items are read to the student and their response is recorded on the survey. The BADDS is useful because children can rate themselves in areas relevant to academic success, such as attention, self-direction, memory, organisation and learning styles.

An example of a completed Brown Attention Deficit Disorder Scale is provided in Figure 3.2 for fourteen-year-old Brian.

Note the same numerical scale as with the Conners' Rating Scales – a T-scale using the same T-score thresholds. The areas measured are:

- *Activation* – Organising, prioritising and beginning tasks like homework and chores. Brian perceives slight difficulty in this area.
- *Attention* – Sustaining attention to task, not being distracted, etc. Brian self-reports a problem in this area (i.e. he is easily distracted and cannot maintain focus).
- *Effort* – Problems relating to a sluggish cognitive tempo, inconsistent work quality, and so on. Brian perceives he has a significant problem with effort.
- *Emotion/Affect* – Brian does *not* report issues regarding the modulation of his emotions, like frustration, anger, sensitivity and anxiety.

Figure 3.2: Example of a Child's Self-Report on the Brown ADD Scale

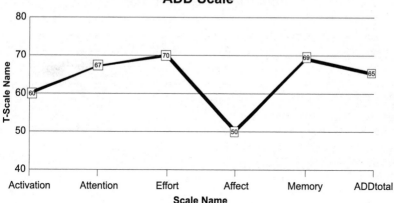

- *Memory* – Generally pertains to recall, forgetfulness and methods used to learn information. Once again, Brian reports a difficulty with retaining information.
- *ADD Score* – Identifies those at risk of ADD without hyperactivity. Brian self-perceives a significant degree of attention deficit disorder.

Gilliam Asperger's Disorder Scale

When there is a query about social difficulties, or the initial conversation repeatedly refers to issues with social connection and social skills, psychologists might employ the Gilliam Asperger's Disorder Scale (GADS).

The GADS consists of 32 statements which can be completed by parents and teachers. The completed ratings yield four subscale scores and one general Asperger's disorder score, known as the ADQ. For ease of communication, the outcomes will be related in a single standard score value, as given in Figure 3.3 for fifteen-year-old Jennifer.

The numerical scale on the left ranges from 50 to 150. ADQ scores greater than 80 are considered as indicating a 'high/probable' chance of having Asperger syndrome, scores between 70 and 79 are 'borderline' and scores below 70 are 'low/not probable'. The first four numbers are specific domains that provide strengths and weaknesses as follows:

Figure 3.3: Example Parent Rating for the Gilliam Asperger's Disorder Scale

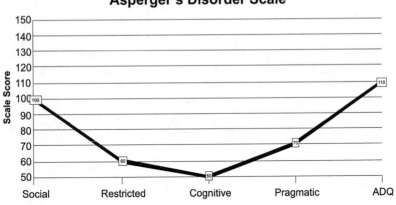

- *Social Interaction (Social)* – Raters measure the student's social behaviours such as cooperating in a group, expression of emotion and awareness of social codes. Jennifer's overall social interaction score indicates significant problems, particularly 'difficulty cooperating in a group', 'difficulty interacting with a peer group', 'not understanding how others feel' and 'lacks appropriate expression of emotion to a given situation'.
- *Restricted Patterns of Behaviour (Restricted)* – Raters measure narrowness of the student's interests, idiosyncratic behaviours, eccentricities, and so on. For Jennifer, this area was rated below statistical significance, indicating that she does not display unusual, eccentric or highly rigid routines.
- *Cognitive Patterns (Cognitive)* – This scale measures specific strengths related to Asperger syndrome, such as excellent memory, focus on a single subject and narrow but extensive knowledge on a particular topic. The rater does not observe Jennifer having unusual knowledge about a specific topic.
- *Pragmatic Skills (Pragmatic)* – Measures understanding of the nuances of social communication, such as social banter, slang and teasing, and the tendency to literally interpret social events. Marginal issues are noted for Jennifer.

- *Asperger's Disorder Quotient (ADQ)* – Identifies the probability of Asperger syndrome. Overall, the rater observes Jennifer engaging in a significant degree of the Asperger-type behaviours measured by this instrument.

Adaptive Behaviour Assessment System

Another type of rating concerns independent living skills, also known as adaptive behaviour. Psychologists may use the Adaptive Behaviour Assessment System, second edition (ABAS-II). As with the other rating forms, the ABAS-II can be completed by both parent and teacher (only the parent form is discussed here). Adaptive behaviour is generally defined as practical, everyday living skills, such as those involved in basic care of self as well as interactions with others. Adaptive behaviour is relevant to the diagnosis of intellectual disability/impairment. There are nine core skill areas (and one optional work domain, depending on the age of the person being rated). These nine skill areas comprise three broad areas of functioning, as well as the General Adaptive Composite (GAC). The raw scores of the rater are converted to a standard score where the average is 100 and the standard deviation 15. Scores which fall below a standard score of 70 are considered 'extremely low'. An example of a completed ABAS-II parent rating is provided in Figure 3.4 for 'Catherine'.

The domain scores are defined as follows:

- *Conceptual* – The specific areas included in this cluster are communication (e.g. speech and language, listening, conversation and responding to questions), functional academics (basic reading, writing and maths required for independent living) and self-direction (the type of self-initiation required to start and complete tasks, such as keeping to schedule, following directions and time management). Parent ratings indicate Catherine has an overall standard score of 78, which is 'well below average'. However, there was significant variation in the areas comprising the conceptual domain, from a very low score of 2 for self-direction (e.g. problems

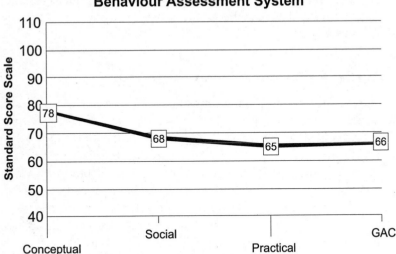

Figure 3.4: Example Parent Rating on the Adaptive Behaviour Assessment System

initiating and completing tasks) to an average score of 9 for communication (e.g. no difficulties with language skills).

- *Social* – The social domain consists of two areas: leisure (e.g. skills related to planning and engaging in recreational activities, playing with others, following rules, etc.) and social (understanding emotions, assisting others and social etiquette). Catherine's standard score of 68 is 'extremely low' with subtest scores of 5 for leisure (not able to play with others, problems following rules) and 2 for social (not understanding how other people feel, not expressing appropriate emotion in a given situation, etc.).
- *Practical* – There are four separate areas which comprise practical. One is self-care, which comprises personal care, particularly eating, dressing, bathing, toileting, grooming and hygiene. A second area is home living – the types of skills needed for the maintenance of one's living area, e.g. cleaning, straightening, organising, performing chores and repairs. The third subset is health and safety, namely health promotion, responding to illness, following safety procedures, using medicines, etc. The final practical scale is

community use, which constitutes understanding and using community resources – public transport, the library, shopping, etc. The overall parent standard score of 65 is 'extremely low'. The observation is that Catherine has significant difficulty with tasks of home living (she cannot perform house chores), is unaware of health and safety issues (e.g. she displays a lack of caution and does not know what to do in an emergency situation) and neglects self-care (she does not maintain personal hygiene). On the other hand, no problems were reported with regard to community use (she understands and can use community resources).

- *General Adaptive Composite (GAC)* – A score of 66 indicates that Catherine engages in far fewer adaptive behaviours than expected of her age group.

Rothwell–Miller Interest Blank

It is fascinating to see how children vary in their identification of future careers. Take for example Patrick. His parents operate and manage a small farm. Patrick greatly enjoys all activities associated with farm management (cleaning and feeding of animals, maintaining farm equipment, purchase of necessary supplies, etc.). As he progresses through secondary school he has already decided that he wants to pursue farming and hopes to study Agricultural Science in college.

By contrast, Lisa is beginning her final year of secondary school. She enjoys school and is not encountering any difficulties with her subjects. As the CAO process is looming, she is forced to consider what she wants to study in third level. When she thinks of college study, she is overwhelmed by the possibilities and cannot pin down her interests to specific courses/careers.

In Lisa's case, it would be useful if the psychologist included a career interest measure. It is important to realise that the purpose of an assessment is not always problem focused (e.g. learning problems or behaviour issues). In Lisa's situation, an assessment could include the career aspect. Also, the cognitive tests described later in this chapter can be useful in guiding the student towards particular higher education programmes (e.g. a high score on visual reasoning tests indicates an aptitude for visual careers, such as engineering, graphic design, fashion or art).

There are numerous methods to explore career interests, all varying in terms of how careers are defined, measured and interpreted. One measure is the Rothwell–Miller Interest Blank (RMIB). The RMIB consists of nine blocks of jobs, with twelve jobs in each block. The respondent ranks each job in each block from 1 (highest interest) to 12 (lowest interest). The test manual includes percentile ranks which are used to show how the respondent's career interests compare to a similar sample of same age students/adults.

Table 3.1 shows the rankings of Martin for each of the twelve categories of vocations.

Table 3.1: RMIB Results for Martin

Occupational Category	Rank
Outdoor (e.g. PE teacher, greenskeeper, landscaper)	1
Mechanical (e.g. machine serviceperson, TV technician)	2
Social services (e.g. psychologist, youth/community worker)	3
Practical (e.g. picture framer, leather worker, dressmaker)	4
Aesthetic (e.g. artist, cartoonist)	5.5
Clerical (e.g. insurance worker, office administrator)	5.5
Computational (e.g. accountant, stockbroker)	7
Persuasive (e.g. advertiser, public relations worker, solicitor)	8
Medical (e.g. surgeon, pharmacist)	9.5
Literacy (e.g. editor, magazine writer)	9.5
Science (e.g. geologist, biologist)	11
Music (e.g. composer, arranger, guitarist)	12

Martin's top four preferred categories are outdoor, mechanical, social services and practical. The practical category would be substantially higher if not for several rejected job titles that could be considered gender specific (e.g. dressmaker) or more antiquated titles (e.g. curtain maker). Martin tended to reject careers that require increasing cognitive and academic complexity, such as in the literacy, medicine, science and computational categories.

Summary of Rating Scales

The primary purpose of all rating scales is to quantify the perceptions and observations of those most familiar with the person being rated; in most cases, the parents and teachers. As noted, there are also self-reporting rating scales that measure the perception of the child him/herself. By providing a numerical metric with statistical guidelines defining if a child has/does not have a problem, the psychologist is more confident in the final conclusions.

Rating scales, however, are not without limitations. Some of these limitations may already be apparent to you. For example, can one purposely rate a child either extremely high or extremely low to obtain services or to prove a point? Yes, although on some of the newer instruments there are scales measuring response bias; this looks to see if the parent/teacher intentionally answers most items in a particular manner. Personally, I believe that the vast majority of respondents approach rating forms honestly, not with the intention of consciously marking all items in a particular direction. The normal process is as follows:

- Does the rater understand the general meaning of the item? If the item states 'has difficulty organising school materials for study/homework', how does the rater interpret this statement (e.g. what exactly does 'organising' mean?)? Once they decide on the meaning of the statement, how do they measure it? This leads to the next issue.
- The child's behaviour is considered with respect to the item and the rater decides on a number. While the ultimate numerical choice is certainly subjective, my belief is that the majority of raters attempt to respond with an honest assessment of the child with respect to each item.

Even in cases where the rater has assigned all maximum or all minimum item values, this does not necessarily imply a conscious attempt on their part to place the child in an extremely favourable/unfavourable light. It may reflect the rater's genuine belief that there are extreme problems or the complete absence of problems.

In some cases, a rating form will contain incomplete or blank items. Again, this does not imply careless responding. It probably means that the rater does not have sufficient information to rate the child. Or, alternatively, they may not understand the statement and so choose to leave the statement blank. This represents another problem with rating scales – some of the statements on rating forms are difficult to interpret. Items may be ambiguous and ill-defined, such as 'is inattentive to social stimuli'. Even a seemingly obvious item like 'short attention span' is open to debate: what exactly does 'short' mean? Or, the rater might understand the statement, but their first response is 'It depends!' In other words, there may be conditions where attention span is not an issue and other situations where attention span is poor. How does the rater assign a number in this case?

A final limitation to rating scales is that most of the scales are developed in other countries, particularly the United States. As a result, some rating statements may be more relevant in one culture but far less relevant in another.

PERFORMANCE TESTS

In this category, children perform a task and their skill is compared to the standard for their age. The tests used in an assessment are individually administered, which sets these tests apart from some of the more familiar educational tests administered in schools (e.g. MICRA-T, SIGMA-T and the Drumcondra tests). With performance tests, there is a strong element of standardisation, both in terms of how the tests are created and how they are administered. The term 'standardisation' means that there is a fairly rigid administration and scoring system.

While performance can be measured in any number of areas, the two key areas in an assessment are the intelligence and achievement (or attainment) tests. Briefly, intelligence tests concern problem solving, logic, speed of responses, memory and abstract/conceptual thinking. The types of tasks on intelligence tests are not typically encountered in everyday life, so the emphasis is on adapting to, and solving, novel problems. On the other hand, achievement tests reflect what is learned in school, particularly the three common pillars of school learning – reading, writing and maths. There are other areas of school learning that can also be included in achievement tests, such as language skills (e.g. oral expression and listening comprehension).

Intelligence Tests

The measurement of intelligence has been one of the more controversial topics in all of psychology. After years of experience teaching and administering these tests, the following personal comments are relevant:

- Intelligence tests indicate levels of cognitive ability. If general cognitive ability is low, it is more difficult for a child to succeed in school. If students struggle in school, it is important to know what their level of ability is so learning materials and expectations can be adjusted in line with measured ability.
- The prediction of success in school or in later career cannot be based on ability alone. One of the most useful axioms in psychology is that performance is a combination of ability and motivation. So, if ability is on the lower end of the scale, a high level of motivation can result in the same level of performance as the opposite combination – high ability and low motivation.
- One can teach the types of reasoning skills that underpin intelligence tests and this can result in modest gains in the underlying abilities. However, benefits tend to be linked directly to the specific task. For example, teaching a child to re-create designs with blocks will result in gains using the exact same materials, but may not result in skill transfer to variations to the task (e.g. recalling the design, by drawing it after a delay, or using blocks with different patterns).
- The abilities measured by intelligence tests are limited to the cognitive domain; there is no assumption that low cognitive ability

translates to low ability in other areas, such as interpersonal skills, emotional maturity, adaptive behaviour (as previously discussed), musical ability or athletic/physical ability.

- The behaviours of a child engaged with a task are as important as the test scores; as noted in Chapter 2, it is significant whether or not the child gives up easily with repetition, they can concentrate and maintain effort, they understand instructions, they demonstrate any strategies during the test, and so on.
- Intelligence tests can provide information about a variety of abilities and variation in these abilities is very useful for school and career planning.
- While outcomes on an intelligence test will probably be similar, even across different psychologists and different tests, this is not always the case. In some instances, significant score variations can occur for a variety of reasons, such as the child's rapport with the psychologist, clinical experience of the psychologist, motivation of the child, noise and distraction levels in the assessment setting, and the type of intelligence test used. All tests have measurement error.

The areas central to most intelligence tests are:

- *Vocabulary*: orally defining words
- *Comprehension*: understanding and explaining various events
- *Pattern analysis*: reasoning with shapes/designs/pictures
- *Memory*: immediate recall of numbers, pictures and patterns
- *Speed*: quickly performing a copying or search task under a time limit

Currently, psychologists usually select from three or four of the most widely used intelligence tests, namely the Wechsler Intelligence Scale for Children (now in its fourth edition), the Stanford–Binet Intelligence Test (fifth edition) or the British Ability Scales (BAS). These tests will be clearly named in the report and the results on all parts of the intelligence test will be described.

The test discussed in this book is one of the most widely used intelligence tests, the Wechsler Intelligence Scale for Children (fourth edition), otherwise known by its acronym, WISC-IV. The WISC-IV is an individually administered intelligence test measuring the cognitive ability of children between the ages of 6 years and 16 years, 11 months. There is also the Wechsler Preschool and Primary Scale of Intelligence for younger children and the Wechsler Adult Intelligence Scale (also fourth edition) for adults. The WISC-IV yields four specific intelligence scores (verbal comprehension, perceptual reasoning, working memory and processing speed) and one general aggregate score (the overall, or Full Scale Score).

Verbal Comprehension

Verbal comprehension (VC) refers to understanding, thinking and expressing oneself with words. Receptive and expressive language are core elements, as is knowledge of words. VC consists of three core subtests:

- *Similarities*: The child is given two words that represent a single idea or concept, and the child is asked how the ideas are connected, for example, 'How are a chair and a table alike?'
- *Vocabulary*: The child is asked for the meaning of an orally presented word, for example, 'What does "enormous" mean?'
- *Comprehension*: The child is given various social, interpersonal, governmental, practical and common sense questions. Questions are longer than the other two subtests and the child is sometimes asked for a second reason to fully assess their verbal fluency. For example, the child could be asked, 'Why do many foods need to be cooked?' One response could be 'To kill germs/bacteria.' If two responses are required, the psychologist would ask, 'Can you think of any other reasons?'

Children and adolescents obtain scores on all three of the above tests. These scores are then aggregated to yield a single verbal comprehension score.

Perceptual Reasoning

The complete antithesis of verbal comprehension, the perceptual reasoning (PR) tests measure non-verbal, visual, spatial and motor skills. If required, the tests could be administered without instructions simply by pointing and gesturing, and the respondent could solve the problem by pointing or constructing the desired model. In other words, language is not a factor, other than the oral instructions regarding how to complete the task.

As with verbal comprehension, there are three perceptual reasoning subtests:

- *Block design*: Here, the child is given three-dimensional blocks, each block consisting of three different colour patterns: all red, all white or half red/half white. They are then asked to re-create a given design as pictured in the test booklet.
- *Picture concepts*: The child is given rows of two, three or four pictures. As an example, one row might contain pictures of a mitten, a pencil and a cat. The row below it consists of pictures of a car, a basketball and a hat. The child scans the pictures in both rows and identifies the theme that connects one picture in the top row with one in the bottom row. In this case, the child selects the mitten and the hat as connected because both are items of clothing. No other combination of pictures is linked in a thematic manner. As each page of pictures is presented, the themes will vary – writing implements, locking devices, signals, objects that float and so on.
- *Matrix reasoning*: The child is given a grid or sequential pattern, with one element missing. At the bottom of the booklet are five options and the child selects the option that fits with the logic of the grid. For example:

Example of a Matrix Reasoning Item

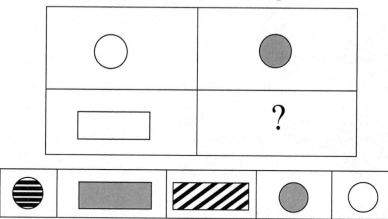

These three core perceptual reasoning tests are then summed to give a single overall perceptual reasoning score.

Working Memory

There are two core working memory (WM) subtests, both of which require one to keep information in immediate consciousness and perform an operation with the input. The two core WM tests are:

- *Digit span*: Here, the psychologist presents a series of numbers, with each series lengthening as the test progresses. The child then repeats the sequence in the order presented. The second part of the task requires the child to recite the sequence in reverse order. For adults, there is a third requirement: the numbers are repeated in order from smallest to largest numbers.
- *Letter–number sequencing*: The child is presented with a random mix of letters (A to Z) and numbers (1 to 9). They must recall the numbers first, in ascending order, then the letters in alphabetical order. So, if given '6 T 3 B' the response would be '3 6 B T'.

The two working memory tests are added to yield a single working memory composite score.

Processing Speed

The final WISC-IV domain is processing speed (PS). The PS tests are timed paper and pencil measures. These tests represent clerical speed and accuracy, ability to perform under time pressure and copying speed. There is some motor aspect, as the visual input is processed and then the response is motoric; that is, the process of copying the mark with pencil onto paper constitutes the motor element. The two PS tests are:

- *Coding*: The child is given a code with a number in the top part and a geometric symbol (e.g. ^ or /) in the bottom. The numbers 1 to 9 each have a unique symbol. Then, in a given time frame, they use the code to quickly assign each symbol to the given number.
- *Symbol search*: In a given time limit, the child is asked to scan a series of shapes (again, various symbols, such as ^, | or ~). The series consists of one or two target shapes and three to five alternatives. The child marks whether one of the two target shapes is exactly the same as one of the alternatives. If it is, they mark 'yes'; if not, they mark 'no.'

As with all other composites, the two processing speed tests are combined to provide a single processing speed score.

Full Scale Score

Once all tests are completed, it is possible to calculate a Full Scale Score. This represents general intelligence, and is an aggregate of the four scores detailed above: verbal comprehension, perceptual reasoning, working memory and processing speed.

Some psychologists present WISC-IV outcomes in both text and/or table form. My preference is to present WISC-IV results (and all other cognitive outcomes) in chart, table and text form. I find the use of a simple line graph effective in communicating all cognitive test results. Figure 3.5 provides an example of Claire's WISC-IV score.

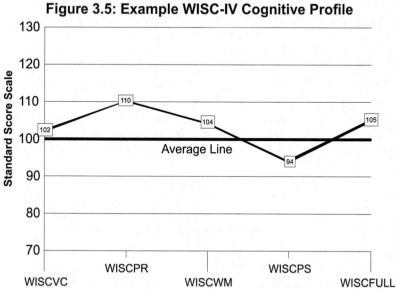

Figure 3.5: Example WISC-IV Cognitive Profile

Table 3.2 summarises Claire's WISC-IV outcomes. All subtests have the same average, which is 10, with the lowest possible score being 1 and the highest possible score 19.

Table 3.2: Claire's WISC-IV Outcomes

Test	Summary of Findings
Verbal Comprehension (WISCVC)	Score of 102 is 'average', indicating that Claire's verbal reasoning ability is at a level expected for her age (e.g. thinking and expressing herself with words; language use/understanding). Claire's subtest score ranges from 9 (oral definition of words) to 11 and 12 (classification of word pairs; understanding long oral questions regarding social/practical knowledge).

(Continued)

Table 3.2: (*Continued*)

Test	Summary of Findings
Perceptual Reasoning (WISCPR)	Score of 110 is 'above average', showing marginally advanced visual reasoning ability (e.g. thinking with pictures, analysing visual relationships). Claire's subtest scores range from 10/11 (identifying themes across rows of pictures, determining pattern logic) to 14 (constructing models with three-dimensional blocks).
Working Memory (WISCWM)	The WM factor is comprised of two subtests, both measuring ability to keep information in conscious awareness and perform an immediate operation with that information. Claire's score of 104 is 'average' and well within the range of performance expected for her age. Her WM subtest scores were 12 (repeating number sequences in forward and backward order) and 10 (immediate recall of numbers and letters in a prescribed order).
Processing Speed (WISCPS)	PS is the ability to quickly scan visual symbols. Claire's score of 94 is 'average'. Her PS subtest scores were 8 (rapidly and accurately copying symbols using a number–symbol code) and 10 (rapidly and accurately scanning symbols to determine a match).
Full Scale Score (WISCFULL)	The Full Scale Score is an estimate of overall cognitive ability. Claire's Full Scale Score of 105 (63rd percentile) shows general cognitive ability in the 'average' band.

The standard score scale illustrated in Figure 3.5 and referred to in Table 3.2 can range from 40 to 160, although scores less than 70 or greater than 130 are rare (roughly 4 per cent of the general population will be above 130 or below 70). A standard score of 100 is the exact average and scores between 90 and 110 are taken as the 'average' band. Some argue that the range from 85 to 115 is 'average', a liberal definition of 'average' with which I would not agree. In any case, Figure 3.5

shows the WISC-IV composite scores (VC, PR, WM and PS outcomes), as well as the Full Scale Score, on the standard score spectrum for Claire's test results.

In Claire's case, all of her WISC-IV outcomes are positive in that no score is 'below average'. Also, there is only a 16-point standard score range from highest to lowest outcome, with all composite scores in the 'average' band; perceptual reasoning would represent a relative strength.

Each of Claire's subtest scores is provided in Table 3.2. Again, the subtest score range can vary from 1 (the lowest point on the scale) to 19 (the highest point on the scale). The exact subtest average is 10. Some psychologists will separately present each subtest score. My preference is discuss the subtest scores briefly within each composite they represent. In many cases, there is not significant 'scatter' (variability) within subtests in a specific domain. Since all tests are statistically connected with one another to form a particular type of intelligence (e.g. verbal comprehension), it is understandable why all tests within a given domain yield similar results; after all, each domain measures related activities. Therefore, in a large percentage of cases, the domain subtest scores show relatively even outcomes.

If there is subtest variation it is usually the same pattern. In my experience, in the verbal comprehension domain, vocabulary tends to be the lowest score while in the perceptual reasoning area, picture concepts often give the highest subtest score. In the perceptual reasoning area, block design requires more motor feedback (e.g. hand–eye coordination) relative to the other two PR tests. Thus, a low block design score coupled with two higher scores on the less motor-involved perceptual reasoning tests may be revealing in terms of fine visual–motor coordination.

The WISC-IV is a classic case of a pyramid. Each subtest represents the foundations on which the next level, the composite, is based. The composites then form the top of the pyramid, which is the overall or Full Scale Score. As with any pyramid, if one of the foundational blocks is faulty, the entire structure is at risk. In the case of the WISC-IV, if a child does poorly on a single subtest, that domain score is lowered, as is the Full Scale Score. For example, a seven-year-old child performs in the 'average' band on most tests, except one – digit span. The child does not understand the concept of backward recall and continues to recall the numbers in the forward direction (even when given several examples of the correct responses). He obtains a low score on this section which lowers the digit span score, which lowers the working memory score, which lowers the Full Scale Score. While there are methods to circumvent this problem (e.g. administer a supplemental working memory test or derive a general ability score where working memory is not included), the interdependency of scores is the take home point.

A major focus of Chapter 4 is different WISC-IV score patterns. WISC-IV scores are essential in the diagnosis of various learning problems. The categories of learning problems applicable can be generically classified by uniformly low WISC-IV scores, uniformly high WISC-IV scores, or significant and thematic score variation within the four domains of intelligence. In the first instance, uniformly low WISC-IV scores, such as those consistently below 85, indicate significant problems across all cognitive skills – problems with language use and understanding, difficulty with visual/spatial thinking, issues with memory and slow processing speed. A uniformly low WISC-IV pattern indicates a general learning disability (again this will be discussed in the next chapter).

The second case is uniformly high WISC–IV scores, or, at least high verbal comprehension and perceptual reasoning scores. If scores surpass the 95th percentile (a standard score of 124), the outcomes are consistent with being 'gifted' and 'talented'. Again, this topic will be elaborated on in Chapter 4.

The final example relates to significant and thematic score variability within the WISC–IV. Some of the more common types of domain score variability:

- *High verbal comprehension and perceptual reasoning scores compared with lower working memory and processing speed outcomes.* Although this is not the only factor to consider, this WISC-IV score variability is common in children with specific learning disability and attention deficits. Verbal comprehension and perceptual reasoning are the two most conceptual and abstract areas whereas working memory and processing speed emphasise memory, attention, and sequencing, all possible risk areas for students with specific learning and attention problems.

- *High verbal comprehension and working memory with relatively lower perceptual reasoning and processing speed scores.* Verbal comprehension and auditory memory are both language-based and the input is auditory. On the other hand, perceptual reasoning and processing speed are both visual and language is minimised. If this pattern emerges, the child may present with a non-verbal learning disability, a problem expanded on in Chapter 4.
- The exact opposite of the previous profile: *Low verbal comprehension and working memory and high perceptual reasoning and processing speed.* This is indicative of specific speech and language disorder, as will be discussed in Chapter 4.

The WISC-IV, by itself, cannot be used to diagnose learning problems. We also need to know whether a child is performing to their age level in all areas related to academic learning: reading, writing and maths. Also, some problems, like dyspraxia, may not manifest in WISC-IV outcomes, hence the need for other tests and other professionals (e.g. occupational therapists or speech and language therapists) to assist in the diagnostic process.

Achievement Tests

In contrast to measures of intelligence are the achievement tests. Whereas intelligence represents novel thinking and problem solving, achievement tests are concerned with what is learned in school; these tests are also known as attainment tests. The most commonly used attainment test is the Wechsler Individual Achievement Test, second edition (WIAT-II).

The WIAT-II is an individually administered test of academic achievement. The age range is from four years of age to adulthood. Like the WISC-IV, the WIAT-II consists of composite scores in reading, mathematics, written language and oral language. The oral language tests are typically not administered by psychologists because (a) language tests are covered in the WISC-IV verbal comprehension domain, (b) additional language testing may be better served in other professional assessments (i.e. by a speech and language therapist) and (c) to save time, as the administration of the entire WIAT-II can last as long as two hours, depending on a number of factors, such as the length of time required by the child to read passages, to answer questions and to complete an essay. The three WIAT areas normally administered by a psychologist in an educational assessment are covered next.

Reading

There are two standard reading subtests – word reading and reading comprehension, discussed further below. There is also a third reading subtest called pseudo-word decoding, which is probably the most optional of the three reading measures. As the name implies, 'pseudo-words' are nonsense words (e.g. 'sloy' and 'hode') that are read by the child. As they are not real words, the purpose of the test is to determine the child's application of phonics to non-English words. As this test is not as central to the reading battery as the other two reading measures, it will not be included in the discussion to follow.

Although not a separate test, an important reading variable – reading speed – can also be derived from the reading comprehension subtest. To do this, the psychologist adds the child's reading speeds across four or five passages and converts them to a reading speed standard score using supplemental tables. The two main reading subtests are:

- *Word reading*: For the younger age groups, this test begins with letter naming and proceeds to pre-reading skills, such as rhyming, discriminating beginning and ending letter sounds, blending, single-letter sound correspondence, and two-letter sound correspondence. For example, the child is given a set of letters – n, u, t, v and p – and is asked to point to the letter that makes the 'puh' sound as in 'pony' or the 'uh' sound as in 'up'.

  The final part of this test is the oral reading of a list of progressively more difficult words. The first words are simple, frequently occurring words (e.g. at, on). The list then moves on to slightly more challenging words (e.g. which, correct, version) and then to less familiar words (e.g. consummate, diphthong). When the test is concluded the psychologist coverts the child's raw score to a standard score by referencing their age group. The standard score is the same metric as discussed with the WISC-V (standard score range of 40 to 160, with an exact average standard score of 100 and the average range between 90 and 110).

- *Reading comprehension*: The main purpose of this test is to assess understanding of what is read. The reading material varies in length from one or two sentences to longer passages, both fiction (e.g. fables and stories) and non-fiction (e.g. science, biography or letters debating a position). The child is asked questions about what they have read, varying from literal detail (e.g. finding a given piece of information) to more abstract questions (e.g. making an inference given the information). They are also asked the meaning of a word in the passage. All of the sentences are read aloud by the child to assess reading fluency in context (since reading a list of disconnected words, as occurs with the word reading test, is not natural reading). In the sentences, there are a number of target words in each sentence that the psychologist will score as correctly read or not correctly read. The psychologist can then calculate the percentage of words correctly read out of the total target words. So, an eleven-year-old might read twenty target words, and correctly pronounce eighteen of them (a 90 per cent accuracy rate).

Written Language

The writing domain consists of two separate subtests – spelling and written expression.

- *Spelling*: The youngest age groups begin with writing their names, writing a letter when given its sound, and writing letter blends when given the blend sound. For example, the child writes the two letters that make the 'chuh' sound as in 'chase'. Subsequently, the child is asked to spell orally dictated words, from simple words (e.g. log, book) to moderate level words (e.g. fluency, patch) to more challenging words (e.g. equinox, chagrin, vestibule).

- *Written expression*: For the youngest age groups, this test begins with writing the letters of the alphabet in order within a given time limit. The next aspect is written fluency, where the child is asked to list as many items as possible given a specific category – words beginning with 'M', things found on a farm, etc. There is a limited time period to generate the list.

  The written expression test includes sentence combination and sentence generation. In the case of sentence combination, the child is asked to combine two existing sentences into one sentence that is well written and means the same thing. Sentence generation is where the child has to describe a picture or summarise information.

  The final aspect of written expression is a sample essay. For children age eight to eleven, a paragraph is expected with between five and ten sentences. The first sentence is started for the child. For older students (twelve to adult), a persuasive essay is required on a given topic.

When the written expression test is completed, all elements of the test are scored and converted to a standard score, like all other WIAT-II measures. In addition to the single standard score, the writing sample of children and older students yields significant information, such as handwriting quality, writing speed and percentage of spelling/grammar/punctuation errors given the total word count.

Mathematics

Like the reading and writing domains, maths consists of two core sub-tests: numerical operations and mathematical reasoning:

- *Numerical operations*: For the younger age groups, the test begins with maths readiness skills, such as identifying one number from others, counting, and writing numbers from 1 to 10. Subsequently, the test covers all basic operations, beginning with single digit computations and moving to larger numbers, and then branching to calculating percentages, fractions, decimals, the value of a constant, simple geometry/algebra, etc.

- *Mathematical reasoning*: For this test, the focus is on problem solving and using a variety of maths applications – measurement, understanding bar charts, calendars, time, money, probability, understanding number sequences and the number line, and word problems.

Like the WISC-IV, the WIAT-II outcomes can be presented in graphic form (see Figure 3.6 for James' profile).

Figure 3.6: Example WIAT-II Profile

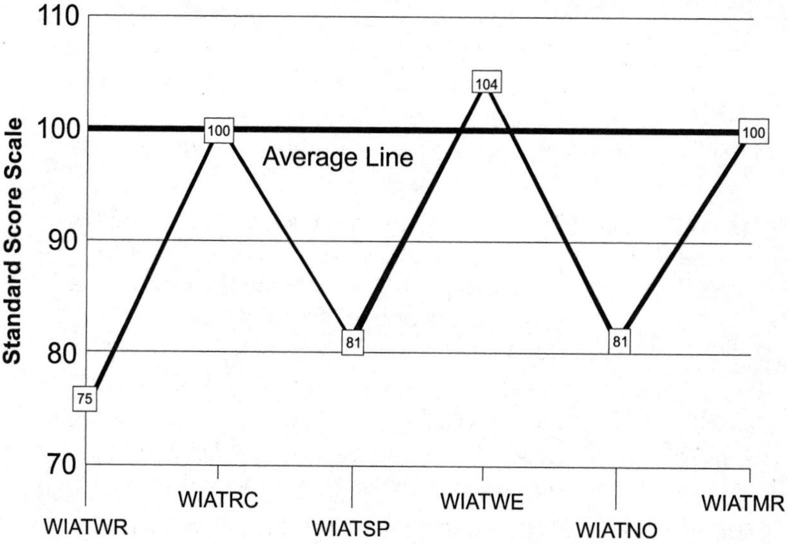

Table 3.3 elaborates on the information provided in Figure 3.6.

Table 3.3: Summary of James' WIAT-II Outcomes

Test	Summary of Findings
Word Reading (WIATWR)	This is a measure of word pronunciation skill. James' WIATWR standard score of 75 (5th percentile) is 'well below average'. That is, James did not recognise as many words as expected of a same age comparison group.

(*Continued*)

Table 3.3: (*Continued*)

Test	Summary of Findings
Reading Comprehension (WIATRC)	This task requires the child to read sentences and passages and answer oral questions about them. James' WIATRC standard score of 100 (50th percentile) is at exact age 'average', indicating he has an age-expected ability to comprehend what he reads.
Spelling (WIATSP)	This test requires the child to write an orally presented word. James' WIATSP standard score of 81 (10th percentile) is 'below average'. Reverse administration was required to achieve a base level of skill, as James miscued on the initial words administered – 'diveing' for 'diving', 'bored' for 'board', etc.
Written Expression (WIATWE)	This test measures a variety of writing skills, such as fluency, sentence combining and generating, and essay development. James obtained a standard score of 104 (61st percentile), which is 'average'.
Numerical Operations (WIATNO)	This is a computational test (e.g. 41 + 14). James' WIATNO standard score of 81 is 'below average' (10th percentile), showing he has difficulty with basic computational skills.
Mathematical Reasoning (WIATMR)	This is a measure of maths concepts (e.g. money, time, measurement and problem solving). James' WIATMR standard score of 100 (50th percentile) is 'average', indicating he has age-expected ability in maths reasoning and applications, such as understanding graphs, money, calendars and word problems.

There is a certain pattern to James' WIAT-II scores which will be discussed briefly in the next section.

Summary and Comment Concerning the WIAT-II Test

A few general comments about the WIAT–II: first, in the core areas of reading, writing and mathematical achievement, the two core subtests can be divided into mechanics and comprehension (see Table 3.4).

Table 3.4: Categorisation of the WIAT-II Tests

Mechanics	Comprehension
Word Reading	Reading Comprehension
Spelling	Written Expression
Numerical Operations	Mathematical Reasoning

The term 'mechanics' refers to the literal, concrete and non-abstract nature of these tasks. Reading or spelling the word 'avaricious' does not require the child to understand the meaning of the word. One must reproduce it given its sound (spelling) or one must interpret the phonics of the word to correctly pronounce it (where do syllable breaks go? What sounds does each combination of letters make?). Likewise, 8 x 4 or 384 ÷ 14 requires a procedural sequence, but not any deeper thinking or alteration to the existing numbers.

By contrast, the comprehension tests require more abstract and deeper-level thinking: what does the word 'avaricious' mean? When reading, the person may read the words accurately, but not understand what was read; certainly understanding text requires higher-level thinking compared to the processes involved in spelling or pronouncing words like 'squandered' and 'abolish'. Essentially, the mechanics of reading involves the correct pronunciation or spelling of the word while comprehension requires an understanding of the meaning of the word.

The same is true with writing. Spelling is a mechanical skill involving phonics – 'u/nee/lah/ter/ul' makes 'unilateral'. One mechanical aspect of writing is punctuation: the child must start each sentence with a capital letter and end with a full stop or question/exclamation mark. By contrast, writing expression also includes abstract elements, such as structure, vocabulary, coherence/unity and depth. To demonstrate a comprehension skill in writing your child must be able to structure an essay with clear paragraphs for each point in a persuasive text. They may sequentially present each argument (e.g. 'First ...', 'My second reason ...', 'Finally ...'). And they are expected to use a varied and reasonably sophisticated vocabulary – another comprehension aspect of written expression. Yet they may misspell words, use incorrect words and fail to capitalise or use correct punctuation (the mechanics of writing).

Maths is no different. A question like 'What is $56 \div 8$?' requires a different level of thinking compared to a word problem like:

Ms Ryan's classroom has eight shelves of books in its bookcase. Each shelf has the same number of books. There are a total of 56 books in her bookcase. How many books are on each shelf?

The mechanics/comprehension divide can be useful in cases where a child scores consistently lower in all of one type of test compared to the other (as will be demonstrated in Chapter 4).

As alluded to earlier, James' WIAT-II outcomes clearly fall into the mechanics versus comprehension divide. He is clearly skilled in all aspects of comprehension across the curriculum – reading, writing and maths. However, his difficulties lie in all mechanical areas – word reading, spelling and numerical operations. This type of pattern is consistent with a specific learning disability such as dyslexia. The only difference is that children with dyslexia may perform at age standard across the maths spectrum – both numerical operations and mathematical reasoning – since maths achievement does not involve literacy. Also, even though the maths reasoning test contains word problems, the psychologist reads the problems to the child, thereby circumventing the issue of reading as it relates to maths word problems.

The second comment is that achievement tests ideally mirror the curriculum. Obviously, if school learning is the focus, then the achievement test should contain items drawn from the school curriculum. When a test like the WIAT is revised, such as the second edition, or the forthcoming third edition, the test producers typically gather feedback from regular users of the test. This reduces the chances that a particular item will be culturally bound and not reflect what is taught in the country where the test is administered. But this does not necessarily eliminate some mismatches between test content and how the material is taught in school. For example, the beginning of the WIAT-II word reading test contains letter-naming questions for six-year-old children. In some early reading programmes, however, the sounds of letters are emphasised; letter names come later. So, when asked to name the letter 'b' a child might say 'buh' but cannot provide the letter name. With prompting and explaining, the child might understand that the task is to simply say the name of the letter, not provide a sound (or character) from a specific phonics programme. If the child cannot name the letter, even after prompting, then the test item does not correlate with how the children are taught early reading skills. If the teaching methods are completely phonic based, the child might not learn letter names. In this situation, a deficit in this skill may not be due to the child's lack of skill, but reveals a mismatch between the test objective and the teaching method. If the psychologist feels this is an issue, the results from the test will be interpreted with caution.

Obviously, many items are universal, such as basic computational skills. On the other hand, the money items on the mathematical reasoning test are bound by the currency in the country in which the test was standardised. Therefore, if the test was standardised in the UK and the coins represent UK currency, the psychologist must devise a method to translate to the common European currency.

Teacher Use of Achievement Tests to Determine Eligibility for Examination Accommodations

There is an increasing trend in which designated teachers in secondary schools use achievement tests to support a student's application to the State Examination Commission (SEC) for reasonable exam accommodations during state exams. The test teachers most commonly use is the Wide Range Achievement Test, fourth edition (WRAT-4). The results of the WRAT-4 are then used to determine whether the student qualifies for examination accommodations.

If a school teacher administers a standardised achievement test and the student's scores are above the score criteria for exam accommodations the parents and student are informed that exam accommodations will not be forthcoming. This may lead to a sense of panic and concern, especially if the same student was awarded these accommodations for the Junior Certificate examination. Let's assume that the same student was previously assessed by a psychologist. The parents can inform the assessing psychologist that their child, who may have been assessed many years ago, in primary school, is not entitled to exam accommodations. Alternatively, if the child was not previously assessed the parents and student may desire an independent assessment. What are the options in these cases?

If the results from teacher-administered achievement tests are above the criteria listed by the SEC this does not mean that different achievement tests will yield the same result. A student's outcomes on achievement tests, even alternate forms of the same test, can differ by 10 to 15 standard score points. Therefore, if one thoroughly investigates achievement, by administering two or three measures of the same domain (e.g. word reading or spelling), a student can be above the threshold on some tests and below it on others.

My advice to parents is to always consider an independent assessment. Even if the student's results on school-administered tests are above the threshold, this does not preclude a parent from seeking an independent and intensive investigation. A psychologist's report will be an integral part of an SEC application. The assessing psychologist will leave no stone unturned in terms of thoroughness; key achievement results can be re-tested with another measure of the same skill. Obviously, however, if all tests are above the required score, then the particular exam accommodation cannot be endorsed.

SUMMARY

In terms of technical development, rating scales and performance tests represent the highest standard of instrumentation available to those conducting assessments. The instruments described in this chapter, especially the performance measures, undergo regular revision to take account of changing cultural patterns, demographics, feedback from test users and, of course, new thinking regarding the domain of the test (e.g. changing theory).

Performance tests are the defining feature of an assessment, as these tests shape, structure and delimit the psychologist's interaction with the child. An educational assessment is not counselling or psychotherapy; there are no open-ended questions, there is no attempt to elicit feelings, explore emotions or identify behaviour patterns. The psychologist follows a clear, procedurally defined format, and the child responds to the material. The data from both performance and rating measures are vital to many diagnostic conclusions, as you will see in the next chapter.

Like a hammer, a scalpel or a paintbrush, performance tests and rating scales are only as good as the one wielding them. Experienced psychologists know how to optimise performance and reduce any negative behaviour patterns that may undermine the entire assessment process. Personally, I find that patience, praise and enthusiasm are essential. For example, within the confines of test protocol and common sense, the child should be given ample time to deliberate; the psychologist should not give the sense that the child needs to move quickly to the next item (obviously when time limits are imposed, this is not possible).

A good psychologist will always be on the lookout for positive observations, such as effort and the use of a spontaneous strategy to solve a problem (e.g. talking aloud when problem solving or rehearsing quietly before repeating a number sequence). When the child displays an adaptive or effortful response to test materials, a good psychologist will be sure to praise. Finally, no matter how many times a psychologist administers the same test, they must display a genuine sense of joy and happiness when a child is successful, especially after dedicated problem solving. The mood and enthusiasm of the psychologist helps to establish a positive atmosphere in an inherently difficult situation for some children.

4

Educational Diagnoses

In the two previous chapters, we covered the most commonly used methods to gather data. The next step is to review all of the data and formulate a conclusion about the problem. In other words, to develop a diagnosis. Herein lies a great source of misinformation and confusion, namely the notion of labels.

LABELS – MYTHS AND REALITY

The diagnostic aspect of an assessment is intimidating for some. People may equate diagnosis with a label. I have experience of parents cancelling an appointment because they do not want their child labelled, or parents reporting that their child is reluctant to attend because of the same concern. If one equates a diagnosis to a label, then, yes, there is a label. If a doctor suggests you use a blood pressure cuff for 24 hours and the results consistently show you have hypertension, then hypertension is a label derived from the blood pressure data. Is this label not vital to your health? If you do not submit to blood pressure assessment you will not know what your risk of heart disease is. Is this not critical, even though you will then carry a label of hypertension?

To a lesser extent the same is true with a psychoeducational assessment. If the conclusion is that a child has a general learning disability, parents and teachers should know this. In the absence of knowing a child's ability to learn, how can one provide realistic instruction? Also, if a clear style of learning is identified, then it is possible to emphasise the child's strength in the teaching–learning process. Even if parents are considering sending their child for an evaluation, the assessment may be delayed or omitted for two reasons: the 'wait and see' approach and the 'we are already working on the problem, so what's the point' attitude. A pattern develops that goes something like this:

Parents might have a concern about their child's learning early in primary school. The parents relay their concerns to the teacher. In responsive schools, the child is provided with learning support without needing a psychological assessment. Several years pass and perhaps there is a sense of improvement.

The student then enters secondary school. She struggles with languages but, in the Irish education system, can take a lower level exam paper (e.g. Ordinary level instead of Higher). She completes her Junior Certificate and may even be granted exam accommodations (e.g. a scribe), all in the absence of knowing the exact problem.

Eventually, somewhere during the Leaving Certificate cycle, the parents decide to have her assessed (she is now seventeen years old). The outcomes of this assessment reveal severe problems in language and literacy, but also clear strengths in certain areas. For example, she is very adept in visual reasoning and maths. Surely this begs the question as to why an assessment was not conducted earlier. There is much that could be done for this student but at seventeen some windows of opportunity are no longer open. Think of the long-term impact on academic self-esteem. Going back to the medical analogy, is it not better to know what the problem is, the severity of the problem, and how to treat a diagnosis of hypertension? The same should apply in this circumstance.

One might think that such examples of delayed or omitted assessments are rare, but this is not the case. In my practice, a significant percentage of Leaving Certificate students attend for assessment for the first time. This is despite the assessment showing obvious problems, problems that could easily have been detected and managed much earlier in the student's educational life.

There are professional discussions about the pros and cons of labelling.** Over the years, I have come to appreciate the true importance of labels, namely:

- Consider the chaos in the absence of labels. Everyone has some problem, we don't know what the problem is, we don't know how much of a problem and we don't know who to provide services to and for what. In the absence of labels, we cannot build knowledge, as there would be no categories to search for patterns, look at themes within groups, test hypotheses, look for differences between groups, and so on.
- The ultimate value of a label is the pursuit of empirically valid intervention programmes. If we have a working hypothesis of attention deficit/hyperactivity disorder (AD/HD), we know the educational settings that promote learning and reduce behavioural difficulties; we know that active, small-group instruction is better than large-group lectures; and we know that 'movement breaks' are required. None of this would be possible if we didn't know the label (or at least the working label).
- A label is really a conduit for relevant services. The special needs aspect of education cannot function without having established rules/criteria that define a 'special need' and at what level on the needs continuum does one deploy valuable and limited resources and services.
- Finally, and perhaps most importantly, the product of an assessment is not always a label. All psychologists who conduct assessments have probably come to the conclusion that one cannot define 'abnormal' without first knowing what is 'normal'. In the case of cognitive testing, there are clear boundaries on the standard score scale that define normality, which is basically 90 to 110. If a child/adult completes all tests and all their scores are above 90, then there is no 'abnormally' low outcome. Obviously, if standard

---

** Jerome Sattler (1988) *Assessment of Children* (third edition), San Diego, CA: Jerome Sattler Publisher, pp. 551–552.

scores were consistently above 110, this would indicate advanced skills. The conclusion is that the student/child is problem free or that their cognitive profile is within (or above) normal limits (much like blood pressure and hypertension: if your blood pressure is normal, you are not hypertensive). Basically, an assessment can just as easily rule out a problem as it can identify one. Although I do not have precise percentages, my best guess over the years is that about 5 to 10 per cent of cognitive outcomes among the people assessed are completely within the 'average' band. It is important to realise that the percentage of normal profiles is much higher in the non-referred population; by contrast, in a practice where assessments are sought because of suspected learning difficulties, the percentage of actual cases exhibiting one or more formal learning disabilities will be substantially higher.

Now that we have overcome the issue of labelling, the next topic is how one classifies the various developmental, learning, behavioural, emotional, motor, physical and social disabilities. Essentially, there are two different classification systems, one psychological/psychiatric and the other educational. There is some overlap between the two, as some educational categories are broad and the psychiatric/psychological system is more specific. For example, one of the educational categories is 'emotional disturbance behavioural disorders'. The sub-categories of this area refer to psychological classifications, such as attention deficit/ hyperactivity disorder, oppositional defiant disorder, depression and anxiety. One common psychological/psychiatric classification system is the *Diagnostic and Statistical Manual of Mental Disorders* (DSM), now in its fifth edition. The DSM-V system will be discussed further in some of the sections to follow.

The classification system that provides the framework for this chapter is the educational disability system developed by the Department of Education and Skills (DES). Specifically, DES Special Education (SP.ED) Circular 08/02 is relevant and can be found on the DES website. SP.ED Circular 08/02 lists twelve disabilities (or special educational needs). In the discussion below I have added one more category, which is not technically a disability: 'gifted and talented'. In reviewing the eleven listed disabilities (the twelfth category is for 'multiple disabilities'), they can be clustered as:

- Cognitive disabilities/talents detected entirely through performance tests
- Sensory and physical impairments requiring medical assessment
- Emotional/behavioural disorders and autistic spectrum disorders requiring psychological intervention (or, in the absence of intervention, knowledge of DSM)
- Motor and language disorders requiring two distinct assessments

Briefly, in the first category, an educational psychologist can use performance tests to diagnose any of the designations in this category. No further assessment is required. The types of problems commonly detected will be amply illustrated later in this chapter as referrals for learning-related problems are the most common reason for assessment. The following categories of learning-based disabilities will be discussed in this chapter:

- Specific learning disability
  - Dyslexia
  - Dyscalculia
- General learning disability
- Comprehension disability
- Non-verbal learning disability
- Gifted and talented – this category is not a disability per se but is included in this group because the identification is based on cognitive tests

In the second category, some of the medical and physical conditions may be inherited, congenital (acquired during pregnancy), perinatal (acquired during the birth process) or post-natal (acquired after birth, e.g. through infections or toxins). Conditions include cerebral palsy, spina bifida and epilepsy. Children with physical and/or sensory disabilities may require specialised equipment (e.g. walking devices, hearing aids and wheelchairs) or may need specialised assistance during the day for basic care needs (e.g. using the toilet, dressing and eating).

The DES circular also refers to visual and hearing impairments to such a degree or severity that specialised equipment is required. For example, a child who has his/her vision corrected with prescription glasses does not qualify as visually impaired. For this category to apply, the child must be diagnosed, typically by an ophthalmologist, with an underlying eye-related condition/disease that may result in significant or total loss of vision. The same is true for a hearing impairment based on an assessment by an otologist or otolaryngologist. Typically, hearing loss must be to the degree that the child cannot hear instruction in a normal classroom setting, even with a hearing aid.

As physical and sensory disabilities require medical assessment, these conditions will not be covered here. This is not to say that children with physical and sensory impairments should not be assessed, as many of the conditions have associated intellectual and academic deficits. Rather, the medical diagnosis takes priority. Also, depending on the severity of the physical/sensory disability, the psychologist may need specialised training in the adaption of test materials or the use of specialised tests. For example, a child with severe motor impairments caused by cerebral palsy will not be able to complete motor coordination activities, such as writing or reproducing designs with blocks. A child with a severe visual impairment cannot interact with visual tests. A child who is severely deaf will require a psychologist who is trained in sign language.

If you feel that your child has learning cognitive deficits secondary to a medical/sensory condition, you should discuss the situation with a psychologist. The basic question is whether your child can meaningfully complete a standardised sequence of tests without adapting the tests or requiring specialised training on the part of the psychologist. If the conclusion is no, then the assessment should be routed to someone who specialises in that particular disability.

The third group – emotional/behavioural (EB) and autistic spectrum disorders (ASD) requiring specialised psychologist intervention – are a common reason for referral. In this category, DSM-V takes precedence and will be discussed below in conjunction with the common problems which constitute EB and ASD.

Finally, in some cases, at least two assessments are required to establish a special need. The most common disabilities are specific speech and language disorder and developmental coordination disorder (also known as dyspraxia).

COGNITIVE DISABILITIES/TALENTS

Starting with the disabilities, there are five possible learning disability profiles (a sixth, specific speech and language disorder, is considered a specific language disorder and is discussed later in this chapter as part of the section on motor and language disorders). Of these five disabilities, the two most frequent are dyslexia and dyscalculia, which both fall within the category of specific learning disabilities.

In Chapter 3, ability and achievement standard scores from the WISC-IV and WIAT–II tests were discussed. We will now refer back to these tests, since the best way to illustrate all of the learning disabilities is to present the cognitive profile pattern associated with the disability. The illustrations given for each have variations on the theme, but the examples provided represent the most obvious case.

Specific Learning Disabilities

Dyslexia

The primary rule for dyslexia is that general cognitive ability is significantly greater than literacy related achievement. A second rule is that maths attainment is often significantly higher relative to reading and writing skills. With these two criteria in mind, a cognitive profile associated with a classic case of dyslexia is shown in Figure 4.1.

Briefly, the first five scores in Figure 4.1 represent the results from the WISC-IV test and the last six scores the results from the WIAT–II test (as explained in Chapter 3). Let us interpret the outcomes for this child. All of the WISC-IV scores are normal, with verbal comprehension (WISCVC) a modest normative strength. With a specific learning disability, there is a presumption of normal general intelligence. This child, Jacob, clearly meets this assumption as his Full Scale Score of

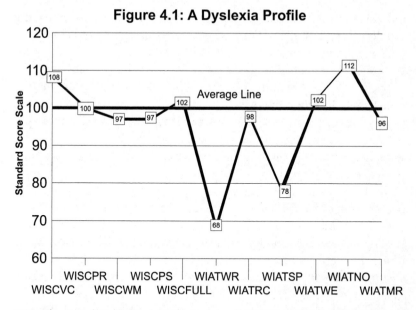

Figure 4.1: A Dyslexia Profile

102 is 'average'. Equally positive is that all WISC-IV domain scores are in the 'average' band.

As for the WIAT results, notice that Jacob's maths skills (WIATNO (numerical operations) and WIATMR (mathematical reasoning), the last two scores in Figure 4.1) are either advanced (NO) or normal (MR). With dyslexia, numerical operations usually score 'average' or 'above average', since numeracy is the antithesis of literacy.

In the reading and writing domains, the mechanics versus comprehension distinction, discussed in Chapter 3, applies to this case. Note the very disparate reading scores with word reading (WIATWR) (mechanics) very low and reading comprehension (WIATRC) (comprehension) close to exact age standard. The same applies to writing: spelling (WIATSP) (mechanics) is very low and written expression (WIATWE) (comprehension) is well within the average band.

This type of profile is typical (with variations) for an individual with dyslexia. Children and adults with dyslexia typically find the two word analysis tests the most challenging. Both word reading and spelling are partners: if you have a printed word, you try to decipher the phonics of the word in order to pronounce it – 'de/ciph/er'. For a dyslexic individual, this process does not come naturally and results in reading problems, such as mis-reading words, inserting extra words into text, omitting words from text and, generally, a slow reading rate. The word 'decipher' could be read as 'deci/fur', 'defer' or 'de/kip/her', for example.

Spelling is word reading in reverse. The word is orally presented, so rather than decoding the printed word, the dyslexic person must take the orally presented word and translate it into a written version. Again, phonics is the cornerstone. How does a dyslexic person write the word 'decipher' when it is orally presented? It could be 'desiphere', 'disiper' or 'decifer', for example.

To understand how difficult this process can be for a dyslexic person, think of a word you have encountered for the first time (take your time and really ponder your recent reading or conversation). Ideally, this word should be unfamiliar and multi-syllabic. Now, write down the word you have identified. Once written, check the correct spelling. Did you find it challenging to translate your mental version to a written one? If so, imagine how difficult it is to write when words familiar to the vast majority of people are not familiar to a dyslexic individual.

The other reading and writing domains (reading comprehension and written expression) are not affected. As there is a presumption of normal intelligence, then the process of comprehension, which is very much connected to general intelligence, can act as a compensator when it comes to understanding what is read and expressing oneself through writing. That is, dyslexic people can use their general intelligence to derive meaning from what is read, using their powers of thinking to overcome mechanical reading errors (adding words not in the text, mis-reading less familiar words, etc.). Similarly, when writing the intelligent dyslexic person may be able to structure an essay, demonstrate reasonable understanding of sentence structure and use a varied vocabulary. However, the mechanics of their writing will often be poor, with incorrect words (e.g. 'aloud' for 'allowed' or 'ware' for 'wear'), spelling errors and grammar/punctuation problems.

Our understanding of dyslexia has grown immensely in the past twenty years. Teachers and parents are more aware of the problems and strengths associated with dyslexia. There are many interventions available, which are discussed in Chapter 6, and the prognosis can be very positive, assuming that the problem is detected sooner rather than later.

Dyscalculia

A second and related disability is known as dyscalculia, which is a specific maths-related disability. An example of a dyscalculic profile is given in Figure 4.2.

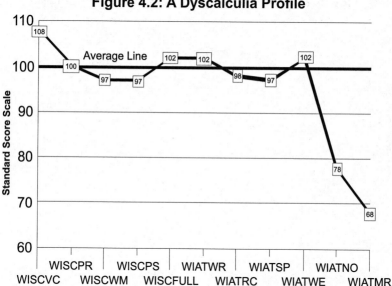

Figure 4.2: A Dyscalculia Profile

For the sake of simplicity, the WISC-IV scores are the same as the previous profile for dyslexia. The obvious difference is the WIAT-II outcomes. Note that the only scores falling considerably below the 'average' band are the two maths scores – numerical operations (WIATNO) and mathematical reasoning (WIATMR). All reading and writing scores are normal. Thus, the problem is specific to numeracy.

In general, students with dyscalculia are of normal intelligence and possess age-appropriate reading and writing skills. However, they have difficulty learning and/or retaining basic maths facts (e.g. 63 – 28, 0.5 + 0.8). Maths applications are also impacted, such as understanding measurement, reading graphs, money calculations and maths word problems.

General Learning Disability

A third learning disability, general learning disability (GLD), is shown in Figure 4.3.

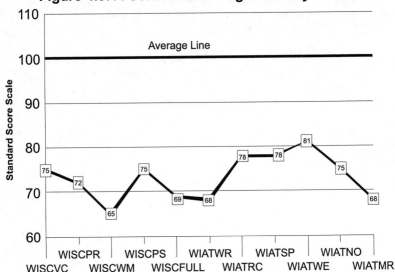

Figure 4.3: A General Learning Disability Profile

The 'general' nature of Sarah's problem is reflected in uniformly low scores; that is, all cognitive outcomes are below the 'average' band. In terms of WISC-IV scores (or any measure of ability/intelligence), the generally accepted definition of GLD is a standard score of 70 or below (less than the second percentile). Sarah would meet the standard for 'mild general learning disability' based solely on her WISC-IV Full Scale Score.

A related term – intellectual impairment – requires the child to also display a similar deficit in adaptive behaviour, i.e. the skills related to practical, everyday living, such as communication, use of resources, understanding of health and safety, hygiene and social interaction. Thus, to determine if Sarah has an intellectual impairment, an adaptive behaviour scale is used, such as the ABAS, mentioned in Chapter 3.

Unlike the specific disabilities of dyslexia/dyscalculia, where problems are reflected in only one area, children with a general learning disability have problems across the curriculum. All reading, writing and maths attainments are lower than age standard. These children may be less likely to participate in class discussion, and they may also find arts and crafts difficult. In general, the long-term educational prognosis can be poorer, as there are fewer strengths to emphasise.

General learning disability is a challenging profile to convey, as it is difficult to be upbeat and positive in light of such uniformly low outcomes. However, there are two possible compensating domains. One is the adaptive behaviour area. If the child possesses age-appropriate adaptive behaviour (e.g. independent living skills), they have a greater chance of full integration into the adult community: work, driving, relationships, etc. If adaptive behaviour is low, then the prognosis is not as positive. The second compensating principal is that *Performance = Ability x Motivation*. *Performance*, in its broadest sense means behaviour, such as academic behaviour, occupational behaviour, recreational behaviour and interpersonal behaviour. *Ability* is the general intelligence required to perform any behaviour, and this element of the equation is defined by a person's overall intelligence score (in this example, 69). So, we know that Sarah may have difficulty performing some activities based entirely on her low ability. What we do not know is her *motivation* to perform. If motivation is low, than the achievement of many basic life tasks will be compromised. On the other hand, high motivation can act as a compensation for low ability, just like low motivation can compromise high ability. In other words, despite low ability, if a person's motivation is high, then there is a greater chance they will achieve basic adult milestones (e.g. independent living).

The finding of general learning disability has significant implications for third-level study. Regardless of motivation, a student with general learning disability will find the increasing complexity and autonomy of college or university education very challenging. Therefore, should a student with general learning disability be encouraged to continue their education into third level? If they have a psychologist's report and recommended interventions in place (e.g. learning support and exam accommodations), the chances are greater that they will be successful in pursuing further education. Again, motivation is critical. However, education beyond the Leaving Certificate is not for everyone and a student (and his/her parents) should not feel pressured to continue with education, especially if the educational profile indicates general learning disability. If they decide to continue education, but do so only because of a sense of family or peer pressure, the college experience will be stressful. Inevitably, difficulties will manifest and the student may fail some modules.

There are alternatives. One is to explore job training. Individuals with general learning disability can be trained in particular areas related to employment. If they want to pursue a particular interest area (e.g. animal care, garden maintenance, or hair and beauty care) or a certain type of employment (e.g. retail or factory work) then these options should be considered. If they want to work in an entry-level position in a shop or factory, why not allow this to happen if it leads to personal satisfaction? Ultimately, the key is to be open-minded and not feel pressured by what other people are doing.

Comprehension Disability

A fourth disability follows the mechanics versus comprehension distinction. Unlike dyslexia, where mechanics are low and comprehension is high, this disability represents the exact opposite: mechanics are high and comprehension is low. So, while a child with comprehension disability has a good grasp of word reading, spelling and straightforward maths questions, their ability to understand what is being read, to express themselves or to apply mathematical concepts to word problems is poor. A classic case of comprehension disability is shown in Figure 4.4.

Clearly, Eoin's profile is very 'spikey', with obvious skills and deficits. The WISC-IV outcomes show two low scores on the abstract/

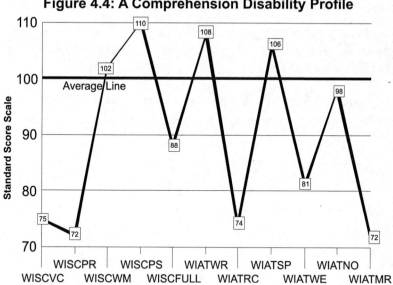

Figure 4.4: A Comprehension Disability Profile

comprehension/reasoning tests, namely verbal comprehension (WISCVC) and perceptual reasoning (WISCPR). However, the other two WISC-IV domains – working memory (WISCWM) and processing speed (WISCPS) – are well developed. Recalling the discussion of the WISC-IV in Chapter 3, it should be clear that working memory and processing speed are more literal, rote and clerical tasks; the student does not have to reason, rather they make an immediate and direct response to the stimuli (e.g. copy shapes, repeat number sequences).

As for WIAT-II outcomes, Eoin performed well in all 'mechanical' domains – word reading (WIATWR), spelling (WIATSP) and numerical operation (WIATNO) – but poorly in all comprehension domains – reading comprehension (WIATRC), written expression (WIATWE) and mathematical reasoning (WIATMR). Combined with the WISC-IV results, Eoin's profile consistently reveals deficits in all aspects of comprehension. There are specific teaching interventions that can be helpful for a child with this profile. The types of interventions suggested will be discussed in Chapter 6.

Non-Verbal Learning Disability

The final cognitive disability discussed here is less common. It is known as non-verbal learning disability or NVLD. An example of NVLD is shown in Figure 4.5.

Figure 4.5: A Non-Verbal Learning Disability Profile

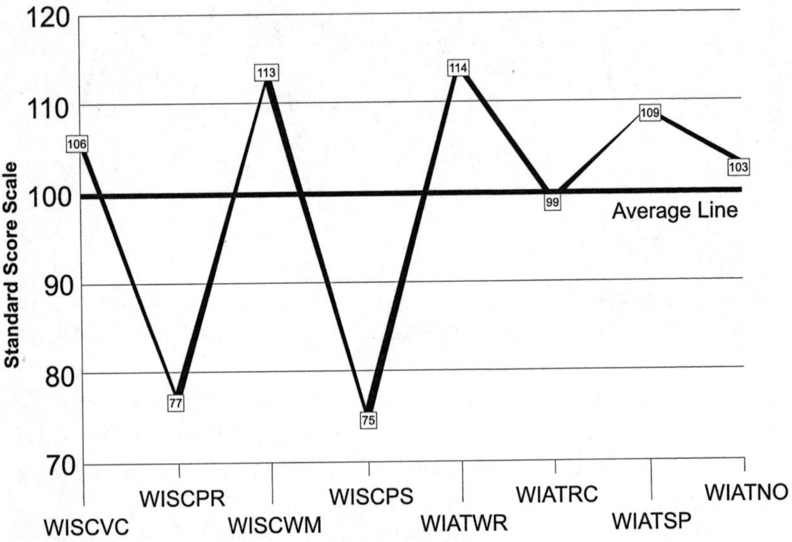

The problem is manifest in the WISC-IV domain scores. Note that the two visual (or non-verbal) areas – perceptual reasoning (WISCPR) and processing speed (WISCPS) – are 'well below average'. On the other hand, the two verbal areas – verbal comprehension (WISCVC) and working memory (WISCWM) – are within, or even above, the 'average' band. Thus, the problem is specific to visually based activities.

Note that Kate's WIAT-II results are generally positive. Most achievement areas reflect verbal skills (e.g. reading/writing as a form of language; basic numeracy through drill and practice). The areas of schooling most likely to be adversely impacted by NVLD are poor handwriting and some forms of maths, particular the more visual maths (e.g. geometry, understanding pattern sequences and visual fractions).

Children with NVLD are considered auditory learners, as the oral language medium is a strength; these children learn better when listening rather than reading. An auditory learner:

- Recalls information better if it is heard rather than seen
- Has difficulty copying from the chalkboard and has poor handwriting
- May be inattentive during visual instruction (e.g. use of charts and overhead projection)
- Makes spelling errors that tend to make sense (e.g. 'meen' for 'mean')
- May not notice visual changes in the environment (e.g. if a small element of change is made to their bedroom)

Logically, children with NVLD often experience difficulties with visual aspects of school, such as arts and crafts. In some cases, there are overlaps with motor coordination problems. Second-level subjects which are most challenging for a student with NVLD are Technical Graphics, Art, Metalwork, Woodwork and Drawing/Design.

Gifted Children

The final cognitive profile discussed here is rather different; Figure 4.6 shows the profile of Mark, who is considered 'gifted'.

If the WISC-IV Full Scale Score surpasses the 95th percentile (which represents a standard score of 124), the ability level of the person being tested is deemed to be in the 'Gifted/Talented' range. Typically, all achievement domains are equally advanced, as is the case with Mark. Parents and teachers might suspect giftedness based on the following characteristics:

- High intellectual curiosity – inquires often about topics and engages in independent learning to satisfy knowledge
- Asks many questions, which tend to be astute and logical
- May be interested in older age groups, as friendship patterns tend to equate with mental, not chronological, age
- May question and challenge authority

- Develops an early reading pattern and continues to read at a level beyond their age peers
- May appear bored or not challenged in class

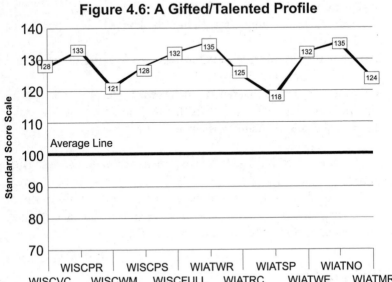

Figure 4.6: A Gifted/Talented Profile

Parents and teachers may be reluctant to have a child identified as gifted/talented. Somehow, this may seem undemocratic and boastful. In fact, just the opposite is true – it is undemocratic, even neglectful, not to have a potentially gifted and talented child identified. In fact, identifying talents is as important as acknowledging deficits. Gifted children require novelty and challenge and may be frustrated by the slow pace of learning in a standard classroom. When frustrated, they may engage in negative behaviour, such as distracting others, not engaging in the work because it is too simple and challenging authority (questioning the material). Therefore, recognising children's giftedness in order to provide a more stimulating educational experience will relieve frustration and result in a much more satisfying school experience. If gifted/talented children are not recognised, their true learning potential may not be realised. It is just as important to provide individualised instruction for a gifted/talented child as it is to provide the same degree of individual education for children with learning-related deficits.

Summary

In this section I have outlined six discrete cognitive profiles. Each profile represents a clear deviation from age standard, five below in one or more areas, and one above. There can also be combinations of profiles, such as a gifted/talented student who is dyslexic. Some outcomes may not be as obvious as in the examples given. Rather, there will be partial problems in some areas.

It is important to understand that cognitive profiles are stand-alone outcomes. There is little room for dispute, as, if accurately derived (i.e. the assumptions of effort and motivation are correct, rapport is good, and the tests are administered and scored properly), the data will reflect genuine skill levels. Some parents might feel surprised that an expected outcome is or is not apparent in test results. For example, parents might assume their child is dyslexic when in fact the outcomes of their tests are all normal. In this case, a suspected problem, such as poor spelling or a general dislike of writing, is not sufficient to be classified as a disability. The assessing psychologist, ultimately, can only rely on the standardised test results to make the case for or against a particular learning problem.

One final comment concerns a profile that represents about 5 to 10 per cent of all cases assessed, and that is shown in Figure 4.7.

The results illustrated in Figure 4.7 represent a problem-free profile. Even though parents or teachers may suspect a problem, standardised tests can indicate the absence of any significant learning difficulties. Take, for example, Figure 4.7. Niamh was referred based on historical difficulties with certain subjects and problems with spelling. However, the results do not indicate a specific spelling problem. If examination of the WIAT written expression test shows that spelling/grammar/punctuation errors are less than 8 per cent of the total word count, then spelling is not an issue. As for ongoing difficulties with a particular language (e.g. Irish or French), these difficulties cannot be accounted for by learning problems. Rather, the issue may be more situational (student–teacher relationship) or motivational (low motivation for the subject).

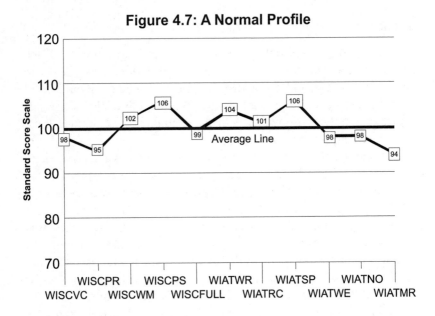

Figure 4.7: A Normal Profile

Emotional/Behavioural and Autistic Spectrum Disorders

This category includes children referred for significant problems that are not specifically learning oriented. Rather, the fundamental problems are emotional issues (outbursts, temper, being easily upset, tearful, sad/moody, withdrawn, etc.), behavioural excess (cannot remain seated, distracts other students, is aggressive towards peers, etc.) and social issues (is not popular with classmates, does not seem interested in other children, has difficulty with peer interaction, etc.). The most common emotional/behavioural and autistic spectrum disorders are discussed below. In this discussion, the emphasis will be on the classification system referred to earlier, namely the *Diagnostic and Statistical Manual of Mental Disorders*, fifth edition (DSM-V).

Performance tests are part of the emotional/behavioural/autistic spectrum assessment. Cognitive assessment is required to rule in or out the learning disabilities/talents discussed above. In my experience, the profiles of children referred in this category are less likely to have any cognitive deficits. Or, there may be a clear cognitive deficit that is associated with a behavioural problem (e.g. a child with significant attentional deficits may have difficulty listening and concentrating when presented with working memory tests).

In some cases, cognitive testing will need to be modified or shortened since the nature of the disability may be counter to the types of skills required to complete mental tests. For example, how can a child with significant attentional deficits complete two-and-a-half hours of sustained tests? Obviously, age plays a factor, with younger children tested for shorter periods.

A second reason for a modified cognitive assessment is the need to explore areas other than pure learning. Thus, rating scales (discussed in Chapter 3) are used to gather relevant diagnostic information. Also, there is the need for a longer parent consultation to cover necessary background details. A single assessment is time limited. The key is to gather only the data that will help answer the most pressing concern, namely the reason for referral.

Let's start with the emotional and behavioural disorders (EBD). While there is much debate and disagreement about the definition of EBD, the general consensus is:

- Children with EBD exhibit problems that greatly impair their ability to function at home, at school and in the social arena.
- There are many types of EBD but a general grouping is:
  o *Internalised conditions*: Children with these problems tend to 'bottle up' their emotions. A particular event or situation may trigger strong feelings of fear, indecision, avoidance and low self-worth. Such a child may be hypersensitive and worried, frequently makes negative self-statements, and usually approaches new activities in a timid, reluctant manner. Some example problems and descriptions of children with internalised conditions include eating disorders, low mood, being self-conscious or easily embarrassed, clinging to caregivers, reduced participation in activities, being fearful, and complaining of aches and pains despite no medical basis for the symptoms.

o *Externalised conditions*: By contrast, children in this category display behavioural excess, such as constant movement, anger, temper tantrums, being easily distracted, trying to dominate others in social and play situations, talking excessively, having difficulty relaxing, being demanding and challenging authority. Emotions and behaviour are far greater than a particular situation demands, namely extreme anger about a relatively small matter, not recognising potentially dangerous situations, not being able to sit still for even a short period of time, and having constant need to be the centre of attention.

- All EBD are diagnosed by psychologists and psychiatrists using a diagnostic system, such as DSM-V.

These two EBD subgroups are discussed further next.

Internalising Conditions

The two common internalising problems in children are depression and anxiety. In children, depression may manifest in the following manner:

- Feeling 'down in the dumps'
- Expressing negative beliefs about the world (e.g. being pessimistic and/or fatalistic)
- Having low self-worth (lack of self-esteem)
- Being insecure or hypersensitive
- May discuss self-injury or have attempted to harm self
- Engaging in excessive self-blame (e.g. 'I'm the reason we lost the game')
- Irritability
- Inability to concentrate
- Fatigue and physical lethargy, such as moving or talking slowly
- Having a reduced interest in activities (parents often report a shrinking interest in hobbies or activities); this includes reluctance to participate in social events
- Increased involvement in non-productive activities (e.g. watching television)

- Sleep disturbance (too little or too much; difficulty falling asleep)
- Weight gain or weight loss
- Loneliness

Specific problems associated with child anxiety are:

- Being nervous, tense or worried
- Being preoccupied
- Recurring worries/thoughts (e.g. death, performing an unacceptable act)
- Being insecure
- Being timid/bashful
- Being fearful
- Being clingy/dependent (afraid to leave caregiver)
- Asking frequent questions about the future
- Being self-conscious
- Frequently complaining about feeling sick or having pains
- Perfectionism
- Nervous habits such as nail-biting or scratching
- High levels of conformity with the expectations of others
- Difficulty concentrating
- Sleep problems
- Avoidance of particular situations (e.g. places, people)
- Intense fear which may consist of feelings of choking, sweating, dizziness, chills, shortness of breath, etc.
- Irritability
- Restlessness
- Fear of losing control
- Repetitive behaviours (designed to reduce anxiety) such as hand-washing

In reviewing the above manifestations of depression and anxiety, one should distinguish between transient and normal manifestations of both anxiety and depression. For example, it is normal for children to worry about a test. Or a child might feel down in the dumps after losing in a sporting event. For the majority of cases, anxiety and depression are fleeting and normal emotional reactions. A comforting discussion with parents or teachers is enough to return to a mentally healthier state. The difference between 'normal' and 'clinical' emotional states is that the negative states are more permanent and less likely to diminish, despite an adult's best attempts to mollify and comfort. The problem is more pervasive and the impact on the child more conspicuous (e.g. they engage in less activity, are more sullen and are less likely to respond to adult requests to change their emotion or engage in some activity). The concerned adult will notice a significant decrease in effort/activity, and an increase in idle, less productive activity (watching television, internet use for recreational purposes, etc.). There may also be an increase in physical symptoms – various aches and pains and medical complaints.

The determination of emotional problems, such as anxiety and depression, is largely dependent on the parent/teacher report. The key for parents is to review the symptom lists above. If you observe a number of these symptoms in your child, then these should be conveyed to the assessing psychologist during the parent interview. There are also rating scales which are specifically devised for measuring parent and teacher perceptions of childhood anxiety and/or depression. One rating scale which covers anxiety/depression is the Revised Behaviour Problem Checklist (RBPC). A completed RBPC is provided in Figure 4.8.

Figure 4.8: An RBPC Test Indicating Emotional Problems

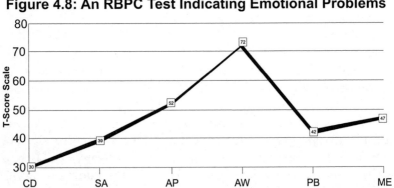

On the RBPC, the highest possible T-score value is 80 and the lowest is 30, as indicated by the T-score scale on the left. Scale scores of 70 or greater are not common and scores of below 60 do not indicate any significant concern. Scores between these two markers (60 to 70) indicate a mild problem, one which should be pursued during the parent meeting.

The outcomes show that the parent (rating a sixteen-year-old female student, Zoe) does not perceive problems in the majority of areas: CD (conduct disorder – Zoe is not disruptive, does not dominate others, does not brag/boast, is not aggressive, etc.), SA (socialised aggression – Zoe does not steal, stay out late or use drugs, etc.), AP (attention problems – Zoe has a normal attention span, can concentrate, can work independently and can finish things, etc.), PB (psychotic behaviour – Zoe does not have strange and far-fetched ideas, etc.) and ME (motor excess – Zoe is not restless and always on the go, does not fidget, etc.). The one very elevated scale score is AW – anxiety/withdrawal. This scale combines items related to mood (depressed, always sad) and anxiety (generally fearful, afraid to try new things, lacks self-confidence, etc.). Given these results, Zoe's parent clearly perceives emotional-type problems, in this case a combination of depression and anxiety. On the other hand, the externalising behaviour problems, such as those in the conduct disorder, socialised aggression and motor excess measures, are not relevant. There is some degree of inattention (attention problems) but difficulties concentrating may be due to general anxiety/depression. In this situation, the parent interview would focus on discussing the RBPC outcomes and gathering further information to corroborate and elaborate on the parent's perceptions.

Externalising Behaviour

Externalising behaviour disorders are best illustrated by two common diagnoses: attention deficit/hyperactivity disorder (AD/HD) and oppositional defiant disorder (ODD).

Attention Deficit/Hyperactivity Disorder

AD/HD is a neuro-developmental disorder resulting in fundamental problems with concentration and completing tasks as well as an inability to control activity level and impulses. Problems with attention span, impatience and excessive activity/restlessness greatly reduce the quality of social, home, academic and occupational functioning. Characteristics associated with AD/HD do not abate with time and continue to interfere with adult functioning (work, relationships, etc.). While all children may be temporarily inattentive, overly active and impulsive, these behaviours in children with AD/HD are far greater than normal age expression. Furthermore, AD/HD is a disorder which manifests across people (with parents and teachers) and environments (home and school), and over time (at least six months in duration). AD/HD is the most commonly diagnosed behaviour disorder in children.

AD/HD has two subtypes and a combined presentation which is relevant when the child has manifestations of both subtypes: (a) inattention and (b) hyperactivity–impulsivity. Significant *inattention* is represented by the following nine manifestations (as indicated in DSM-V, published in 2013):

- Often fails to give close attention to details or makes careless mistakes in schoolwork or during other activities (e.g. overlooks or misses details, work is inaccurate)
- Often has difficulty sustaining attention in tasks or play activities (e.g. has difficulty remaining focused during lectures, conversations or lengthy reading)
- Often does not seem to listen when spoken to directly (e.g. mind seems elsewhere, even in the absence of any obvious distraction)
- Often does not follow through on instructions and fails to finish school work, chores or duties in the workplace (e.g. starts tasks but quickly loses focus and is easily side-tracked)
- Often has difficulty organising tasks and activities (e.g. has difficulty managing sequential tasks, has difficulty keeping materials and belongings in order, is messy, has poor time management skills, fails to meet deadlines)

- Often loses things necessary for tasks or activities (school materials, pencils, books, tools, wallets, keys, mobile phones, etc.)
- Is often easily distracted by extraneous stimuli
- Is often forgetful in daily activities (chores, running errands, keeping appointments, returning calls, etc.)

The second group of symptoms relates to *hyperactivity and impulsivity*, as observed by the following nine markers:

- Often fidgets with or taps hands or squirms in seat
- Often leaves seat in situations when remaining seated is expected (e.g. leaves his or her place in the classroom)
- Often runs about or climbs in situations where it is inappropriate (for older individuals, this may be limited to feeling restless)
- Often unable to play or engage in leisure activities quietly
- Is often 'on the go', acting as if 'driven by a motor' (e.g. unable to be or uncomfortable being still for an extended time, as in restaurants, class, meetings, etc.)
- Often talks excessively
- Often blurts out answers before questions have been completed (e.g. completes people's sentences, cannot wait turn in conversation)
- Often has difficulty awaiting turn (e.g. waiting in lines)
- Often interrupts or intrudes on others (butts into conversations, games or activities, may use other people's belongings without asking or receiving permission, etc.)

If one can identify a majority of these behaviours in one category, but not the other, then the term is either 'predominately inattentive presentation' or 'predominately hyperactive–impulsive presentation'. If significant behaviours are noted in both categories, the term is 'combined presentation'. Many people will recognise attention deficit disorder (ADD) and attention deficit (AD), which is the same as predominately inattentive presentation or inattentive type. All of these designations represent a single group with the same problem. Likewise, if the problem is hyperactivity–impulsivity (without inattention) the common term in the general population is 'hyperactive' or hyperactivity disorder. Typically, children who are inattentive but not hyperactive are easier to manage because there is no behavioural excess. In fact, inattention may be missed because it can be covert in the form of daydreaming and not completing work due to being quietly off-task.

While some of these behaviours may be present some of the time, the key is that the behaviours associated with a clinical condition like AD/HD interfere with, or reduce the quality of, social, academic, home or occupational functioning. Through careful interview, and in conjunction with all other data, it should be reasonably clear if the behaviours associated with AD/HD result in a significant reduction in the quality of life.

Over the years, our understanding of AD/HD has been refined. With the fifth edition of the DSM (DSM-V), published in 2013, there are three important changes that should be noted:

- One of the most fundamental changes is the recognition that AD/HD continues through adulthood, although its manifestation is obviously different for adults compared to children. There is greater awareness that AD/HD does not abate in adults; rather, the presentation changes and continues to impair adult functioning. This is clearly reflected in how the symptoms now include references to adult functioning such as 'often leaves seat in workplace', 'restlessness' and 'forgets to pay bills'. Likewise, the symptom 'often has difficulty organising tasks and activities' includes possible impact on older individuals, namely 'poor time management' and 'fails to meet deadlines'.
- AD/HD is now classified as a neuro-developmental disorder. This represents a change from the earlier edition of DSM, where AD/HD was classified as a 'disorder first diagnosed in childhood'. The new categorisation reflects the increasing body of evidence that AD/HD is a neurologically based disorder. The 'developmental' aspect means that AD/HD is usually first evident in childhood.
- In DSM-IV, it was stated that the onset of symptoms was before the age of seven. In DSM-V, there is greater recognition that onset may be later than age seven but is manifest by age twelve.

How would rating results support a diagnosis of AD/HD? Figure 4.9 shows the results of an RBPC teacher rating for a seven-year-old boy, Conor.

If we look at Figure 4.9, we see that the two most elevated scales are attention problems (AP) (short attention span, cannot concentrate, cannot work independently, does not finish things, gives up easily, etc.) and motor excess (ME) (always on the go, cannot sit still, fidgets, etc.). The high AP rating indicates that Conor has problems with concentration and completing tasks while the high ME rating indicates over-activity and impulsivity. All other scale scores are not statistically significant.

There are different modes of intervention for children with AD/HD. In some cases, treatment involves medication while in others behaviour management programmes are implemented at home (parent training) and in the classroom (common methods to reduce AD/HD in the classroom context). There are also child-related interventions, especially self-monitoring. Some of the more common treatment programmes for children with AD/HD are presented in Chapter 6.

Figure 4.9: An RBPC Rating Indicating Attention Deficit/ Hyperactivity Disorder

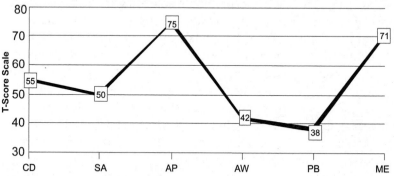

Oppositional Defiant Disorder

Another common behavioural disorder is oppositional defiant disorder (ODD). Children with ODD are typically far more angry, irritable, touchy and hostile towards others when compared to the normal developmental pattern of these emotions. In DSM-V, the main features of ODD are:

- Has problems controlling temper
- Is argumentative
- Is stubborn
- Blames others for mistakes
- Purposely annoys others
- Appears hostile, angry and/or sullen
- Defies or refuses to comply with rules or requests
- Is touchy and/or irritable
- Denies misdeeds
- Often pushes adults to limits, tests patience

In general, children with ODD are hostile towards authority figures. Hostility is expressed in the form of arguing and inflexible persistence with respect to getting what is desired. They are reluctant to compromise and engage in constant whining and persistent disagreement until the battle is 'won'. There are also a number of other factors associated with ODD:

- Although ODD is most commonly noted first in the family context (e.g. within the parent–child relationship), its significance is increased if oppositional features are observed in school. If ODD is observed in the home but less so in other situations, then there is a greater likelihood that family factors may be the root of the problem (e.g. harsh parenting, inconsistent limits, marital discord or parental mental health problems). On the other hand, if oppositional behaviour is observed in different situations (home and school) it is more likely a temperamental feature of the child and, in this case, a formal diagnosis of ODD is relevant.
- Usually, there are signs of ODD in preschool years in the form of a negative temperament (e.g. crying frequently, not being easily consoled).
- While some episodic temper, anger or hostility is evident in most children, the pattern is more stable and impairing for a child with ODD.

How might ODD manifest in parent and teacher ratings? Recall the Conners' Rating Scale described in Chapter 3. Briefly, it consists of a parent and teacher form; the T-score range is 38 to 90, with T-scores greater than 65 indicating that the raters perceive a statistically significant level of the particular area being measured. Parent and teacher ratings relevant to ODD, for ten-year-old Seán, are presented in Figure 4.10.

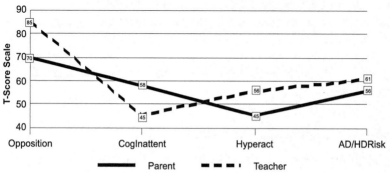

Figure 4.10: Conners' Rating Results Indicating Oppositional Defiant Disorder

Looking at Figure 4.10, note that only the opposition scale is elevated, with all other scale scores below statistical significance. That is, both parent and teacher observe Seán breaking rules, challenging authority, not complying with rules, being easily annoyed and angered, etc. There are no significant problems with academic work, inattention and over-activity.

Treatment of ODD usually involves an understanding of family relationship patterns. A psychologist might explore family dynamics to determine if there is a particular family process that is creating tension and hostility. Also, certain forms of therapy, particularly cognitive behavioural therapy, can be effective in helping the child better understand the roots of anger and to learn more positive methods of expressing feelings. Again, some of the more common techniques to treat ODD are discussed in Chapter 6.

Summary

Emotional and behavioural disorders are challenging for parents and teachers to manage. Also, the actual course of a problem can move from externalised to internalised, making treatment more complex. For example, a child may first show signs of an externalising disorder. As time passes, and anger and frustration build, their mental state may become more internalised (emotional). Children with AD/HD can show this course. For example, a youngster may be described as inattentive, easily distracted, impulsive and over-active. If these problems are not dealt with early, children with AD/HD may wonder why their behaviour is out of control, why they are not reaching goals, and why getting along with others is difficult. They may become increasingly frustrated, angry and defeated. A sort of learned helplessness may set in and this may manifest as one of the internalising problems discussed above (e.g. depression).

Autistic Spectrum Disorders

Autistic spectrum disorders (ASD) are fundamentally a problem with social interaction and social communication. A second problem is the narrow and unusual manner of play, behaviour and speech. There are a group of ASDs that are referred to as 'autistic disorder', 'Asperger disorder/syndrome' and 'pervasive developmental disorder not otherwise specified'. The use of the word 'spectrum' is important given the wide variation in presentation of symptoms, from mild to moderate to severe (the severe category is by far the lowest percentage of the total ASD population).

In terms of development, the earliest sign of an autistic spectrum disorder may be the disinterest an infant shows during the social–emotional bonding period. They may show a dislike for affection (e.g. when cuddled, they may arch away from their caregiver) and socialisation. Autistic infants are typically described as 'good babies' because they can entertain themselves for long periods and do not cry or place demands on parents. ASD toddlers continue to be indifferent to others. They tend to have a fascination with inanimate objects, such as light switches, toy parts, door handles and washing machines (to name a few). Speech and language development is generally restricted and/or atypical (e.g. small speaking vocabulary, repeating certain words and phrases). Speech may be characterised by repetition of words, sounds and jingles (called echolalia), and an unusual voice quality (high pitch, squeaky, dysfluent (i.e. unusual rhythm, so that volume and tone change from the start to end of sentence), etc.). Or, they may be able to speak clearly, but do not spontaneously talk. It is well established that the amount of speech and language the autistic child develops by age two is a good predictor of later adjustment.

When socialisation is required, such as when commencing school, autistic children do not relate in the same way as other children. It is in the socialisation and play arena that some of the core characteristics of autism emerge. For example, they may show little interest in companionship and greater involvement with objects and solitary activities (e.g. playing imaginary games alone). In terms of socialising, an ASD child will either not be interested in connecting with another child or will not have the social skills to interact (e.g. not showing interest in another, not recognising another person's feelings, and being unable to understand non-verbal cues like frowns, tears, anger or smiles). Overall, autistic children show a general lack of interest in companionship, such that they seem 'alone', self-absorbed and only interested in their inner world.

In terms of play, autistic children may entertain themselves for long periods engaged in repetitive and non-imaginary play. The activities and interests of ASD children are described as peculiar and repetitive, even non-functional. For example, the child may continually repeat a certain activity (e.g. align a long row of cars, break the line, re-align the cars, etc.). Preoccupation with parts of toys is evident (e.g. repetitively pushing the play button on a tape recorder). There is little in the way of imaginary play (e.g. giving a doll a cup of tea). As the ASD child develops, narrowed interests may be seen in the continued pursuit of one activity (e.g. performing the same activity on the playground) and a significant dislike for any activity that is directed by others, etc. They may be fascinated with facts, schedules and statistics.

Autistic children often have unusual motor and speech mannerisms, such as hand flapping, unusual postures, rocking, a peculiar gesture or an atypical vocal sound. They may flap their hands, make an intense grunt, pace, or do any combination of unusual movements and sounds. These unusual motor behaviours are technically known as 'stereotypies'. Autistic children require 'sameness' as changes in routine may cause great distress. Sometimes a new sound, or a new item of clothing, will also lead to a very negative reaction. They tend to require a rigid adherence to specific routines.

On a positive note, higher functioning ASD children often show particular talents (e.g. a highly developed memory and recall for specific topics of knowledge, computational skills, exceptionally detailed drawing abilities, or a good understanding of machines). The combination of a narrow range of interests and exceptional memory often leads to extremely well-developed factual knowledge.

Diagnosing Autistic Spectrum Disorders

The latest research (as developed in DSM-V) breaks the diagnosis of ASD into two main categories of symptoms:

- Persistent deficits in social communication and social interaction across multiple contexts, as manifest by all three of the following:
  - Deficits in social–emotional give and take, ranging from abnormal social approach and failure of normal back-and-forth conversation to lack of interest in others, restricted emotions and failure to initiate or respond to social interaction
  - Deficits in non-verbal communicative behaviours used for social interaction, ranging from abnormalities in eye contact and body language, and deficits in understanding and use of gestures, to a total lack of facial expressions
  - Deficits in developing, maintaining and understanding relationships, ranging from difficulties adjusting behaviour to suit various social contexts and sharing in imaginative play or in making friends to absence of interest in peers
- Restricted, repetitive patterns of behaviour, interests or activities, as manifested by at least two of the following, currently or historically:

- Stereotyped or repetitive motor movements, use of objects or speech (e.g. simple motor stereotypies, lining of toys, flipping objects, echolalia, idiosyncratic phrases)
- Insistence on sameness, inflexible adherence to routines or ritualised patterns of verbal or non-verbal behaviour (e.g. extreme distress at small changes, difficulties with transitions, rigid thinking patterns, greeting rituals, need to take same route or eat same food every day)
- Highly restricted, fixated interests that are abnormal in intensity or focus (e.g. strong attachment to or preoccupation with unusual objects, excessively circumscribed or perseverative (restricted/repetitive) interests)
- Hyper- or hypo-reactivity (i.e. either over-reacting or not reacting to an abnormal amount of a particular condition, such as noise or temperature) to sensory input or unusual interests in sensory aspects of the environment (e.g. adverse response to specific sounds or textures, excessive smelling or touching of objects, visual fascination with lights/movement)

For ASD, the above behaviours are usually noted early in development but may not be fully expressed until social demands exceed limited capacity (such as when the child commences school). Or, for older individuals, behaviours may be partly compensated for by learned strategies (e.g. avoidance or removal of self from particular situations, such as an area of the school yard).

There are a number of other points to consider regarding ASD:

- General level of intelligence is an important factor in determining the severity of the disorder; children with higher levels of intelligence typically have a milder presentation whereas lower levels of intelligence are associated with a more severe form of ASD.
- ASD can be part of other genetic and chromosomal conditions (e.g. Down syndrome).
- Children with intellectual disability may show signs of ASD. In this case, the psychologist will state whether ASD coexists with intellectual impairment.

As an educational psychologist's focus is diagnostic, he/she will need to investigate how an ASD appears in objective sources, such as rating scales. One of the most commonly used rating scale for ASD is the Conners' Comprehensive Behaviour Rating Scales (CCBRS). The Conners' Rating Scale discussed in Chapter 3 is a related instrument, but does not have the scope of the CCBRS. The CCBRS consists of almost 200 items which measure parent and teacher perceptions of a child's learning, behavioural and emotional functioning. In Figure 4.11 the parents of Elizabeth rate her behaviour, including some of the main categories of EBD and ASD we have just covered. Again, the scale is a T-score with a range of 30 to 90 and with T-scores greater than 70 indicating the perception of a significant problem.

Figure 4.11: Conners' Comprehensive Behaviour Rating Scales Results Indicating Autistic Spectrum Disorder

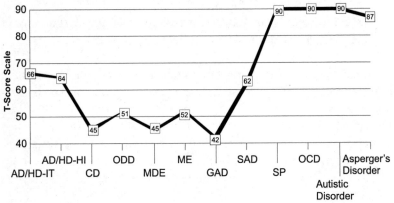

By now, you should recognise some of the acronyms used in Figure 4.11, such as AD/HD (either IT (inattentive type) or HI (hyperactive/impulsive)), CD (conduct disorder) and ODD (oppositional defiant disorder). In this case, the AD/HD scales are marginally elevated while CD and ODD are not perceived as problems. The next two scales relate to the emotional/behavioural disorder domains of depression (MDE – major depressive episode) and mania (ME – manic episode). Depression has been discussed above. Mania is defined by an elevated mood, incessant talking, agitation and non-stop energy in bursts. The two scales that follow measure anxiety, noted in two separate categories: (a) gen-eralised anxiety disorder (GAD), which manifests as worry, difficulty sleeping, poor appetite, edginess and muscle tension; and (b) separation anxiety disorder (SAD), which is worry about being alone or separated from family members. In the case of Elizabeth, emotional problems are not reported. The last four scales are all very elevated. These scales are:

- *Social Phobia (SP)*: In this area, the parents perceive significant problems with social connection; Elizabeth has difficulty with peer interactions and tends to avoid social situations.
- *Obsessive–Compulsive Disorder (OCD)*: Parent ratings indicate that Elizabeth has a repeated thought or idea, which may be upsetting and which she cannot stop thinking about. She might engage in repetitive/ritualistic behaviour (e.g. plays with toys in same fashion).
- *Autistic Disorder*: The very elevated score in this scale is due to a high rating for items like 'repeated body movements over and over', 'is preoccupied with parts of objects', 'limited interests/stuck on one thing' and 'trouble interacting with others'.
- *Asperger's Disorder*: This scale contains the same item set as the Autistic Disorder Scale. The difference is there are fewer items in the Asperger's Disorder Scale which reflects the more positive prog-nosis associated with Asperger disorder relative to autistic disorder. In the section to follow, the relationship between Asperger syn-drome and autism is discussed.

All of the most elevated scale scores relate to Elizabeth having an ASD. Social phobia and obsessions/compulsions all fit with the general per-ception of ASD. In Chapter 6, techniques to improve social connection are discussed. Educational interventions, such as resource teaching, social skills training and a special needs assistant, are also relevant to ASD and will be elaborated on in Chapter 6.

Asperger Syndrome and Autism

Research over the past fifteen years has led to significant revisions in ASD diagnosis, which are reflected in major changes from DSM-IV to DSM-V. One of the most significant changes is that Asperger syndrome (AS) is no longer a separate diagnosis in DSM-V. Rather, Asperger syndrome is now a form of ASD. This particular change deserves further comment.

Previously, the only distinction between AS and autism was that with AS, there was no delay in language development. The idea was that AS represented a 'higher functioning' form of autism. For example, researchers, in rating forms and in books, emphasised the strengths of a narrow focus and intense interest in a particular subject. That is, it was accepted that a person with AS would demonstrate extremely good memory skills and this, combined with an over-focus on a narrow topic, would result in highly developed knowledge in a particular area (a type of insect, Latin names of plants, the mining history of a particular country, astronomy, etc.). In fact, some highly regarded academic professors could potentially fit this description. In any case, the symptoms of AS were recast as strengths and resulted in far more positive outcomes at least in terms of career development and work satisfaction relative to those with autism.

However, when language was delayed, the prognosis was poorer and autism was the diagnosis. Essentially, autism was considered to be 'low functioning' (less communication) and Asperger syndrome was considered 'high functioning' (more language and communication). Now, the degree of functioning defines the child's place on the spectrum and no attempt is made to distinguish Asperger syndrome from autism. Essentially, the degree of verbal/language ability defines a child's place on the spectrum as either low or high functioning. So, if a child has a diagnosis of autism and a WISC-IV verbal comprehension score of 94 there would be no significant difference between him/her and a child with AS; both are 'high functioning'. Both children would share a common set of symptoms – difficulty with social interaction, problems with communication and conversation, and odd or eccentric behaviours and/or speech.

MOTOR AND LANGUAGE DISORDERS

The two final educational diagnoses concern motor and language problems. The most recognised motor disability is known as developmental coordination disorder (DCD), also known as dyspraxia. The most common language disability is specific speech and language disorder.

These two diagnoses require separate assessments. With regard to specific speech and language disorder, a child can only meet all relevant criteria when assessed by both a psychologist and a speech and language therapist. As for dyspraxia, there is some dispute over what assessments are necessary. Current practice allows for either psychologists or occupational therapists to diagnose dyspraxia separately, without the need for an assessment from the other. However, I would argue that assessments from both are essential. This is discussed further below.

Dyspraxia

Consider the task of tying a shoelace. If you have ever tried to teach a child how to tie their shoe, you will realise the complexity of the task. One must have a 'schema' as to what the completed product should look like, referred to as 'ideation'. Once the mental framework is in place, there is the next step of planning – what movements does one make and in what order – to complete the task. Finally, one executes the plan. All three components must be closely linked and occur rapidly and smoothly. With dyspraxic children, there are errors in the process (e.g. a faulty idea or problems sequencing the movements) or in the connection between the components. Thus, the teaching of a skill like tying a shoelace or using a knife may occur slowly and with more difficulty. A child with dyspraxia may encounter a number of difficulties:

- They may be late in attaining motor milestones (e.g. sitting up, walking or catching a ball).
- They frequently bump into or drop things.

- They have difficulties with activities of daily living, such as pouring a drink, using a knife, tying a shoe and buttoning a shirt.
- They are not able to match same age peers in ball sports, such as throwing or catching a ball.
- By virtue of their coordination problems, they may not be selected for games.
- They may have problems with writing/drawing – messy, disorganised, lines slanted, letters uneven, difficulty staying within lines when colouring, etc.
- They do not run, climb, hop or throw like same-age peers.
- They lack muscle tone; muscles may appear underdeveloped.
- They can be messy, disorganised and forgetful.
- They may experience problems with visual, perceptual or spatial tasks (e.g. writing sentences off-centre, not understanding proper space and distance around people, such as standing too close to others).
- They often hesitate before executing a motor movement (e.g. they may consciously stop, pause and concentrate for a second before executing a physical activity).
- They often have poor posture.
- They may be defensive to touch.
- Their activity level may be excessively low (withdrawn, listless) or high (hyperactive).
- They may be socially excluded (due to difficulty with physical games).

As mentioned above, current practice allows for psychologists and occupational therapists to diagnose dyspraxia separately and without the need for two separate assessments. Indeed, some psychologists might feel that a single psychological assessment is sufficient to determine dyspraxia. Alternatively, occupational therapists might argue that the results of their assessment alone are sufficient to make a diagnosis of dyspraxia. I argue that both assessments are required to properly diagnose dyspraxia for the following reasons:

- I do not believe that a psychologist can determine whether a child's 'motor performance [is] substantially below expected levels' (an essential diagnostic criterion) without using specialised tests of motor functions. Usually, these tests (such as the Movement Assessment Battery for Children) are administered by occupational therapists and not psychologists. Also, the main tests used in psychological assessments do not have significant motor components (other than handwriting and some visual motor tests).

- None of the most commonly used rating forms used by psychologists have scales specific to coordination (note that in all previous scales discussed there is no scale measuring motor coordination). That is, a psychologist cannot use an existing rating scale (at least not one with adequate technical standards) to demonstrate low parent/teacher ratings on a coordination index. This provides further support for the specialised nature of dyspraxia and the need for an occupational therapist's assessment.

- Likewise, an occupational therapist must know whether a child's coordination problems significantly interfere with activities of daily living or academic achievement (another essential diagnostic criterion). This requires the use of academic achievement tests, which are administered by psychologists. Although it is no longer a clause in DSM-V, there was a previous stipulation that coordination problems must be below chronological and *mental* age. The issue here is that low motor coordination may be due to generally low intelligence; if this is the case, the diagnosis of dyspraxia is not made unless the coordination problems are in excess of what is typically associated with intellectual impairment. However, one does not know a child's mental age without knowing their level of intelligence, another hallmark of a psychoeducational assessment.

If a child is diagnosed as dyspraxic, ideally from both psychological and occupational therapy assessments, what help is available? The key figure in the treatment process is the occupational therapist, who can advise on programmes for home and school implementation. Typically, these are a series of motor coordination exercises. Children with dyspraxia may also be provided with adaptive equipment which can be used to overcome specific problems (e.g. a special computer with an adapted keyboard or special materials to teach fine motor skills).

Specific Speech and Language Disorder

The final educational diagnosis is that of specific speech and language disorder (SSLD). Children with SSLD have non-verbal ability in the average band or higher but their skill in understanding or expressing themselves through the medium of spoken language is severely impaired. The diagnostic criteria for SSLD is:

- A non-verbal ability score of 90 or above. Non-verbal ability, using WISC-IV, is the perceptual reasoning (WISCPR) scale. Perceptual reasoning tests are non-verbal or use minimal language; in fact, one could administer these tests through gestures, without any language, if required. The child responds to visual input by either motor response (constructing a design with blocks) or pointing to pictures that are logically connected or fit with a given design. No language is required in the response, and the language involved in task instructions can be translated via gestures. Therefore, it makes sense that a child with a language disability would perform within the 'average' band on tests that do not involve language. This is the basis for this criterion. If a child scores low on visual tests as well as language tests their problem is more generalised and not specific to language.
- Clinical Evaluation of Language Fundamentals assessment by a speech and language therapist which places performance in one or two main areas of speech and language development at least two standard deviations below the mean. The Clinical Evaluation of Language Fundamentals (CELF) is a test specific to speech and language therapists, much like the WISC-IV or British Ability Scales are specific to psychologists. This is why a speech and language assessment is required in the diagnosis of SSLD. Like all major tests, the CELF has domain scores, such as expressive, receptive, language content, language memory and core language. These domain scores are expressed in the same metric as WISC-IV and WIAT-II, with the exact average standard score (100). The standard deviation of the test is 15. Thus, the requirement that the score be 'two standard deviations below the mean' translates to a standard score of 70 or below. If one of the CELF domain standard scores is 70 or lower, the child meets this requirement.

- SSLD is not due to hearing impairment, emotional/behavioural disorders or speech delays/difficulties. This final criterion, therefore, is to rule these alternative diagnoses out. For example, if a child meets the diagnostic criteria for AD/HD, SSLD cannot be considered a primary problem. The hearing impairment rule-out is very specific with decibels given for 'normal hearing range'. If a child is diagnosed as having a hearing impairment, SSLD is ruled out.

As for speech delays/difficulties, there are subtle types of language problems that do not qualify as SSLD. The nuances of language and its development are the remit of speech and language therapists. However, we will briefly discuss the main points here. Most parents are aware, in a general sense, of the milestones for the development of speech, beginning with eye contact, babbling, cooing and crying. Before twelve months, infants are typically making partial speech sounds (e.g. 'bah' and 'dah'). Soon after, there are clearly articulated words, which are followed by more and more words. By eighteen months, two-word utterances are made in both declarative ('mean dog') and question ('where dog?') formats. Around age two, longer and more sophisticated sentences begin (e.g. 'I want more drink'). Expressive language continues to mature and by age four most adult-like grammatical structures are fully formed.

Perhaps the most common reason parents first become concerned about their child is the failure of a toddler to meet language milestones. There may be a complete lack of speech (e.g. no clearly articulated words by eighteen months), minimal vocabulary, difficulty finding the right word, jumbled syntax (confused order of words) or articulation/pronunciation problems (failure to correctly produce speech sounds, such as consonant sounds or consonant blend sounds). Alternatively, there may be problems in the speech mechanism (oral motor responses which control voicing, accent, etc.) which result in mis-articulations. The most common speech and language concerns are:

- Delay in attainment of speech/language milestones
- Articulation/pronunciation problems (e.g. certain percentage of words are distorted: 'airspoon' for 'airplane', 'fye' for 'fly', etc.)

- Lisping
- Whispering
- Struggling to communicate ideas
- Overly simplified grammar, vocabulary and sentence type for given age
- Confused morphology (e.g. 'I runned' for 'I ran')
- Disorganised syntax (e.g. 'seatbelts safe you keep')
- Difficulty finding the correct word, which can result in the constant repetition of a phrase (e.g. 'the thing goes here')
- Misunderstanding verbal instructions (the child frequently receives a different message from the one intended and one which would be correctly identified by most children)
- Frequent use of gestures instead of words

A cognitive profile of a child with SSLD is the exact opposite of a child with NVLD, at least in terms of the WISC-IV results. SSLD could be considered a verbal learning disability, whereas NVLD is a non-verbal learning disability. So, the WISC-IV/WIAT-II profile for a child with SSLD, such as Matthew, could look like the chart in Figure 4.12.

Figure 4.12: An Example of a Verbal Learning Disability (SSLD) Profile

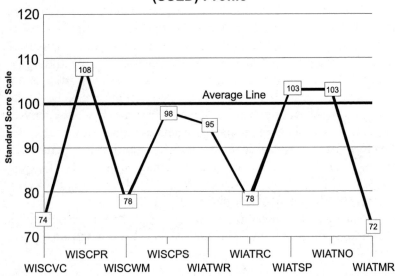

Looking at Figure 4.12, as expected, problems surface in both the WISC-IV and WIAT-II tests. For example, with regard to the WISC-IV outcomes, the two visual (non-verbal) areas – perceptual reasoning (WISCPR) and processing speed (WISCPS) – are 'average'. In contrast, the two verbal areas – verbal comprehension (WISCVC) and working memory (WISCWM) – are 'well below average'. Thus, the problem is specific to language. As Matthew's WISC-IV perceptual reasoning score is greater than 90, this particular case meets the first criterion for SSLD.

In the WIAT-II tests, the outcomes generally resemble the comprehension disability profile provided earlier. This is due to some WIAT-II tests having a heavier language load than others, either more language in the instructions and/or more language required in the response. Thus, WIAT-II reading comprehension (WIATRC) and mathematical reasoning (WIATMR) have greater language loads than word reading (WIATWR), spelling (WIATSP) and numerical operations (WIATNO).

Like dyspraxia and occupational therapists, the main professional in the treatment of SSLD is the speech and language therapist. A child with SSLD will benefit from regular visits to a speech and language therapist. The therapist can also provide remedial programmes for home and school use. Educational psychologists can also recommend specific teaching programmes to assist in the development of language comprehension. Again, the specific methods will be elaborated on in Chapter 6.

SUMMARY

After reading this chapter, it is hoped that you better understand the common educational and psychological problems that impact on school progress. My belief is that parents should always follow their intuition. If you have a concern, consider taking your child for an assessment. If a problem is clear from the results, then you know what it is and what can be done to help.

My attitude is that whatever the outcomes of an assessment, the situation is 'win–win'. If there are no problems, or at least nothing overly worrisome, then the win is that school progress should not be an issue. Or, at least, there are no learning, attentional, motor, emotional, behavioural or social problems indigenous to your child that could explain low school outcomes.

If there is a problem, such as any of the disorders/disabilities mentioned in this chapter, then you now have an explanation and can develop a new understanding in dealing with the issue at hand. For example, if the problem is dyslexia, then weak written expression skill is no longer considered 'laziness' but rather reflects a genuine problem. Your child is not misspelling words on purpose or because they simply do not pay attention to detail. No – writing problems reflect the core symptom of dyslexia. A true understanding of the core issue will benefit child and adult, again a clear win–win.

It is important to realise that the problems discussed in this chapter can co-exist, such as AD/HD and ODD, or dyslexia and ADD, or dyslexia and dyscalculia. For example, autism and general learning disability (or intellectual impairment) often overlap (roughly 75 per cent of children with autism also have an intellectual impairment).

When a child has two or more disabilities, the prognosis tends to be less positive, at least regarding school and later adjustment in adult life. That is, a child with AD/HD who does not have any form of learning disability is more likely to develop more effective compensation strategies, which will lead to more favourable school results. If their intellectual ability is normal then they might be able to use their general ability to achieve higher grades in the absence of age-expected concentration levels. On the other hand, a child with both AD/HD and a general learning disability tends to have poorer educational outcomes. A negative loop occurs such that concentration is poor which reduces the window of opportunity for learning. And, to make matters more difficult, when the window is open and the child receptive, learning does not come easily. This negative loop continues to spiral downward, making school extremely challenging.

It is also important to note that some psychologists will more thoroughly assess some areas relative to others given their personal expertise and experience. There is only so much time one can devote to data collection. Inevitably, something may be missed. Therefore, it is important that you clearly articulate the reasons for bringing your child for assessment during the parent interview.

I believe the information provided in this chapter will help all prospective consumers of assessments to better understand what to expect and how psychologists use test/rating outcomes to formulate conclusions. I realise there are many graphs in this chapter. However, these outcomes (usually presented in table format) will be provided in your child's psychological report so it is important that you have a basic understanding of standardised tests/ratings. Hopefully, this goal has been achieved.

A PARENT'S VIEW

Below is a summary of one family's experience of the assessment process.

At two years of age, our son, Paul, was referred to the HSE after the public health nurse identified a speech and language problem. Due to a long waiting list, we decided to have a speech and language therapist assess Paul through her private practice. He was diagnosed with a language delay.

Eventually, he was assessed by two different psychologists in the HSE. The assessing psychologists noted Paul's difficulties relating to his peers (e.g. isolated play and occasional aggression to peers – hitting, slapping, kicking and bumping into children). The psychologists suggested Paul may have an autistic spectrum disorder. As his behaviour was only mildly in the spectrum and because there were other emotional and behaviour issues that had yet to be formally investigated, ASD was never formally diagnosed.

All individuals involved with Paul noted how active and inattentive he was; in the professional reports, there is frequent mention of his short attention span, intermittent attention, restlessness, inability to remain seated and impulse-guided behaviour (bumping/pushing children).

In the absence of a clear diagnosis, we had Paul assessed by a psychologist in private practice. The results consistently indicated AD/HD. Given the danger to himself and others, a special needs assistant (SNA) was recommended and sanctioned. Paul also obtained the maximum allowable resource hours.

In the intervening years, Paul has made academic and behavioural improvements. He was recently re-assessed and his AD/HD continues to be significant. He also has elements of autistic spectrum disorder (difficulties relating to peers, anxiety/worry, adherence to routines and great upset if the routines are altered, narrow range of play, etc.).

Our current worry is that Paul may not get the resources that have helped him in the past two years. We initially understood that the private psychologist who assessed Paul could recommend resources and an SNA and that these provisions would be retained throughout primary school. Now, we are told that Paul needs an additional assessment (through the HSE). We are also concerned about recent cutbacks and wonder how Paul will manage if his SNA or resource time is reduced or removed.

5

Post Assessment – The Report

The psychological report that follows an assessment is a vital document. The report is usually provided to the parents and/or the referral agent, such as your child's school principal, resource teacher or general practitioner. Reports recommending educational supports will also be reviewed by personnel in the Department of Education responsible for overseeing that particular area. For example, if reasonable accommodation for state examination is recommended, the report will be routed to the State Examinations Commission of the Department of Education and Skills. If resource hours are recommended, the report will be directed to the Special Educational Needs Organiser affiliated with your child's school.

Reports normally have a shelf life of three years. Cognitive profiles are not stable. A problem evident in young children may be insignificant in three or more years. In fact, some argue that a diagnosis of dyslexia cannot be confidently made unless the assessment outcomes are repeated at some later point (such as one year later). The timing of an assessment/report is also important, especially with regard to the CAO application process. If the assessment/report occurred more than 24 months before the CAO application in February of the student's final year in secondary school, it will need to be updated.

The actual length, structure and content of a report will vary. I have seen reports that are just two pages in length and others which are 25 pages long. The actual length depends on how much detail is provided regarding the tests used, how extensive the parent interview was, how many sources and assessment methods were used, how long the analysis is, and how many recommendations there are. The recommendations can be very lengthy if the psychologist provides great detail about teaching methods and materials.

Since the psychologist's report is fundamental to an assessment, it is necessary to discuss it further. The remainder of this chapter outlines the actual sections and content of a report, using my report format as a guide. While the actual names of report headings may be different for your child's report, the spirit of the section is the same.

PSYCHOLOGIST'S REPORT: SECTIONS AND CONTENT

Identifying Information

Most reports begin with identifying information, such as the example below:

****

Name: Jane Doe
Address: Seaview, Small Town, Ireland
Date of Birth: 12 January 2002
Age at Testing: 11 years, 10 months
Date of Evaluation: 20 November 2013
Date of Report: 24 November 2013
School: St Michael's N.S., Small Town
Class: Fifth

****

There is little need for further expansion as this material is self-explanatory. Note that the age of testing is given in years and months, as the most well developed standardised tests have norm groups divided into three-month age brackets. In this case, Jane Doe will be compared with the performance standards of children between the ages of 11 years, 8 months and 11 years, 11 months.

Some psychologists might include more information, such as 'Name of Teacher' and 'Name of Parents'. Otherwise, this section is reasonably standard.

Reason for Referral

The key topic here is why the child/adult was referred for assessment. Normally, this is one or two sentences, such as 'John was referred due to concerns about lack of progress in school' or 'Barbara was referred for psychological assessment due to behavioural issues at school and home'. The section may also include the referral route, such as who initiated the referral (e.g. teacher, parents or general practitioner) and any previous contact with the psychologist or agency.

In some cases, children are referred by schools and there is a section on their referral form which lists the reason for referral. On some forms, this consists of general categories, namely 'Learning', 'Behaviour', 'Emotional' and 'Other'. Typically, there is a section for the referring teacher to add any additional information that will guide the assessment process. The psychologist may choose to summarise the key points in a referral form in the reason for referral section of their report. The reason for referral must be concise since the later sections will elaborate more precisely the issues in question.

If parents make direct contact with a private psychologist, the initial phone call is very important. During the initial phone contact, the psychologist will ask questions to determine the general reason for referral (e.g. learning disabilities). Sometimes, parents will be specific, suspecting a particular problem (e.g. dyslexia, dyspraxia or AD/HD). Or, parents might mention an educational (e.g. struggling with Irish, can't concentrate, not academically progressing), behavioural (e.g. often in trouble at school and home) or social issue (e.g. does not relate well with peers). These details are sufficient to guide the type of assessment required to answer the referral question.

The main themes in assessments are (a) cognitive problems (see the discussion on cognitive disabilities and talents, including specific speech and language disorder in Chapter 4), (b) adaptive behaviour (see Chapter 3), (c) career preferences (see discussion on the Rothwell–Miller

Interest Blank in Chapter 3), (d) motor skills (see the discussion on dyspraxia in Chapter 4) and/or (e) social–emotional–behavioural problems (again, covered in Chapter 4). Each of these areas can be a reason for referral, as gleaned from the information gathered during initial contact with parents and teachers and the pre-referral forms. These themes can then be combined or isolated as the most general reason for an assessment. So, when writing the reason for referral section, one might see variations on these five categories. For example:

****

REASONS FOR REFERRAL

The reasons for a *consultant educational psychologist's assessment* are:

• Determining Luke's cognitive profile
• Providing recommendations based on the profile obtained

****

The first bullet point tells us that the assessment is cognitive. By default, this means that the referral is based on suspected learning problems. The term 'cognitive profile' refers to standardised test results on cognitive performance tests. In Chapter 4 we discussed the most common cognitive profiles.

The second bullet point illustrates the close link between assessment outcomes and recommendations. Obviously, the outcomes will determine the recommendations, so the two are closely interwoven, yet separate. A practical way of interpreting the reason for referral section is, firstly, 'what is the general area being assessed' and, secondly, 'what do we need to do now that we know the outcomes'.

The first bullet point may include variations, such as:

• Determining Luke's cognitive and social–emotional–behavioural profile

This expands the assessment to include methods designed to cover the social, emotional and behavioural domains. Recall that the Conners' Comprehensive Behavioural Rating Scale, mentioned in Chapter 4, measures a parent's/teacher's perceptions of a child's social–emotional–behavioural functioning. There are a number of different rating scales that can be used, which will be named by the psychologist, with outcomes provided in some format (table of rating outcomes, text or both).

- Determining Luke's cognitive and adaptive behaviour profile

The inclusion of 'adaptive behaviour' indicates the use of an adaptive measure, probably to determine whether there is intellectual impairment.

- Determining Luke's cognitive and career profile

The career element may be relevant for Leaving Certificate students and for those in third-level education. The rating system used to measure career interests will be named and explained in the report.

Evaluation Procedures

As the name implies, this section of the report lists the methods used to gather information. This section lists the specific methods used to collect information, such as behaviour observations, parent interview and review of records. An example evaluation procedures section is provided below:

****

EVALUATION PROCEDURES

Cognitive Tests:

- Wechsler Intelligence Scale for Children, fourth edition (WISC-IV)
- Wechsler Individual Achievement Test, second edition (WIAT-II)

Social–Emotional–Behavioural:

- Conners' Comprehensive Behaviour Rating Scale – Parent Form
- Conners' Comprehensive Behaviour Rating Scale – Teacher Form

Informal Measures:

- Behaviour observations
- Parent information

****

One can infer from the headings that (a) the cognitive tests will be used to determine learning strengths/weaknesses and (b) the social–emotional–behavioural domain includes emotional/behavioural disorders (EBD) and autistic spectrum disorders (ASD). The 'informal measures' are two of the most common subjective methods discussed in Chapter 2. Each area will have a separate section in the report body.

Test Results/Outcomes

Typically, the results are separated by area, with one section for cognitive outcomes and one for social–emotional–behavioural outcomes in cases where both areas are assessed. A typical cognitive outcome section is provided below.

****

COGNITIVE OUTCOMES

Figure 5.1 summarises Rory's outcomes for cognitive tests.

If a graphic depiction of the cognitive tests is not provided, the psychologist will have a table or text description of the cognitive results. The results illustrated in Figure 5.1 are explained in Table 5.1.

Figure 5.1: An Example Cognitive Profile

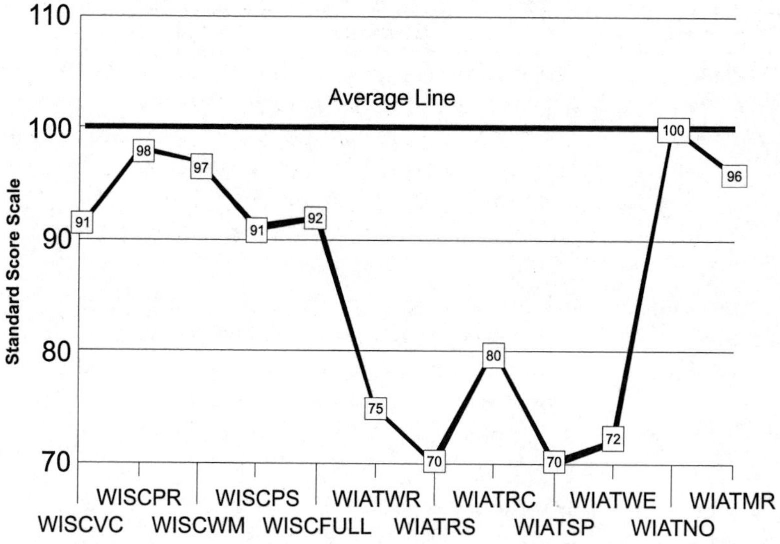

Table 5.1: An Explanation of Rory's Cognitive Profile

Test	Summary of Findings
Verbal Comprehension (WISCVC)	Score of 91 is 'low average' and shows close to age-expected verbal reasoning ability (e.g. thinking and expressing self with words; oral language). Subtest scores range from 7/8 (oral definitions of words; social/practical knowledge) to 10 (classification of word pairs). The subtest average is 10.
Perceptual Reasoning (WISCPR)	Score of 98 is 'average' indicating age-appropriate visual reasoning ability (e.g. thinking with pictures, analysing visual relationships). Score range of 9 to 10 shows age-appropriate skills across a variety of visual tasks: reproducing models with three-dimensional blocks, understanding pattern logic and identifying themes across rows of pictures.

(Continued)

Table 5.1: (*Continued*)

Test	Summary of Findings
Working Memory (WISCWM)	WM involves keeping information in conscious awareness and performing an immediate operation with the information. Rory's score of 97 is 'average'. His subtest scores were 10 (immediate forward and backward recall of numbers) and 9 (immediate recall of numbers/letters in a prescribed order).
Processing Speed (WISCPS)	PS involves rapid scanning of visual symbols. Both tasks are paper and pencil speed tests. Rory's score of 91 is 'low average'. His subtest scores were 7 (quickly copying shapes) and 10 (quickly and accurately discriminating between similar looking shapes).
Full Scale Score (WISCFULL)	The Full Scale Score is an estimate of overall cognitive ability. Rory's FSS score of 92 (30th percentile) shows general cognitive ability in the 'low average' band.
Word Reading (WIATWR)	This is a measure of individual word pronunciation skill. Rory's WIATWR standard score of 75 (5th percentile) is 'well below average'. Lengthy reverse administration was required to establish a base level of word reading ability, as Rory miscued on start point words (e.g. 'invite' for 'invade', 'now' for 'know' and 'engine' for 'enjoy'). He laboriously decoded each word.
Reading Speed (WIATRS)	The WIAT includes supplemental tables which allow for the conversion of total reading time (across four WIAT-II reading comprehension passages) to standard scores. Rory's WIATRS standard score of 70 is 'extremely low'. In fact, if not for a truncated score range (that is, there are no standard score values less than 70), Rory's RS standard score would be significantly lower, as his total reading speeds were far slower than the raw score values associated with a standard score of 70.

(*Continued*)

Table 5.1: (*Continued*)

Test	Summary of Findings
Reading Comprehension (WIATRC)	The WIATRC task requires the child to read passages and answer oral questions about them. Rory's WIATRC standard score of 80 (9th percentile) is 'below average'. Thus, his ability to read for meaning is below the level expected of a same age comparison group. He correctly read 22 of 25 target words across five oral reading samples. Thus, his ability to read words accurately is enhanced when reading connected text compared to reading words in isolation.
Spelling (WIATSP)	Rory's WIATSP standard score of 70 (2nd percentile) is 'extremely low'. A sample of his errors include 'rigth' for 'write', 'jumed' for 'jummed' and 'larg' for 'large'.
Written Expression (WIATWE)	Rory's response to the WIAT-II written expression exercise is provided below. His WIATWE standard score was 72.
Numerical Operations (WIATNO)	This is a computational test (e.g. 41 + 14). Rory's WIATNO standard score of 100 (50th percentile) is at exact average showing age-expected computational skills (e.g. 604 − 396, 0.6 + 0.7).
Mathematical Reasoning (WIATMR)	This test measures maths concepts (e.g. money, time, measurement and problem solving). Rory's WIATMR standard score of 96 (39th percentile) indicates age-expected maths reasoning ability (understanding charts/graphs, money and word problems, etc.).

****

Figure 5.1 and Table 5.1 provide both visual and text presentations to help the report reader understand the test outcomes. Example items in some areas are given to illustrate the difficulty Rory had with particular test items, namely the WIAT-II reading and writing measures. Rory's response to the 'essay' section of the WIAT-II written expression test would usually be provided at the end of the report. For clarity, we include it here:

****

RORY'S WRITING SAMPLE

A writing sample was obtained using the *WIAT-II written expression format* (prompt A – the writer is given the intro, 'My favorite game is ...' and asked to write five to ten follow-up sentences). Rory's writing sample is provided below (words in parentheses are intended words):

> My favorite game is ... mishen (Mission) 6. i lik it becuse you can get rockit lorh (launcher) too shot (shoot) poles (police) helecoter. you chead (create) three poeple. there are mishea (missions) and when you shout (shoot) some one brool (blood) come frome the body.

Comment

- Handwriting is easy to read (in block form).
- There are sixteen spelling/grammar/punctuation errors. Thus, *the total error rate is 44 per cent* (any error rate greater than 8 per cent is considered significant).

****

After cognitive outcomes, the social–emotional–behavioural observations are presented (if this domain was assessed). Using the Conners' Comprehensive Behaviour Rating Scales, an example of this section for Rory is outlined below:

****

SOCIAL–EMOTIONAL–BEHAVIOURAL MEASURE

Conners' Comprehensive Behaviour Rating Scales (Parent and Teacher Forms)

The Conners' Comprehensive Behaviour Rating Scale is a detailed rating form which measures adult perceptions of a child's learning, behavioural and emotional functioning. There are a number of CCBRS outcomes and interpretations but the essential results pertain to 'content scales' and 'DSM-V scales'. Figure 5.2 provides parent and teacher outcomes for the major content scales (not including subscales) that are common to both parent and teacher forms. The scale is a T-score, with a total scale range from 30 (lowest possible) to 90 (highest possible), with any T-score above 70 considered 'very elevated'.

Figure 5.2: Example CCBRS Content Scale Results

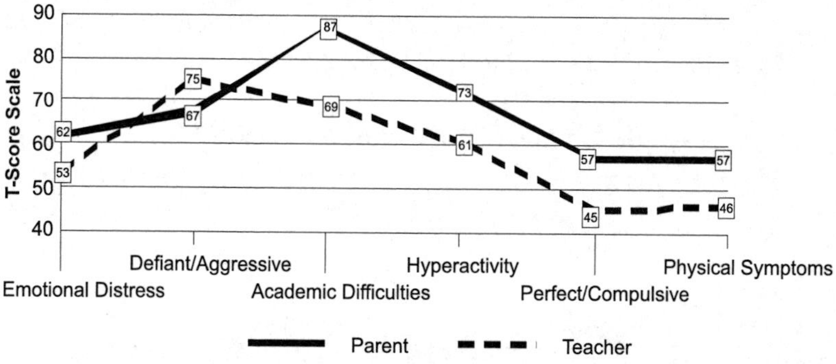

The CCBRS includes many content scales. A sample of six of these scales is provided next:

- *Emotional Distress (ED):* Neither his parents nor his teacher rate Rory as emotionally distressed. The total ED score is slightly elevated in his parents' rating due to their concerns about his social interaction and low academic self-esteem.

- *Defiant/Aggressive Behaviour:* This scale is significantly elevated based on Rory's tendency to argue and say hurtful things to other people.
- *Academic Difficulties:* This scale is significantly elevated and indicates that his parents and teacher are concerned about Rory's difficulties with basic academic skills, especially reading and spelling (these concerns are corroborated by Rory's WIAT-II results).
- *Hyperactivity:* His parents rate Rory as very active, restless, prone to interrupting others, impatient and fidgety, and say he does not remain seated for long. Slightly less over-activity is observed in school.
- *Perfectionistic/Compulsive Behaviours:* Neither Rory's parents nor his teacher perceive problems in this area.
- *Physical Symptoms:* Again, this scale is well below statistical significance.

In addition to the content scales, parent and teacher ratings can be interpreted using the *Diagnostic and Statistical Manual of Mental Disorders* (DSM-V), as outlined in Figure 5.3.

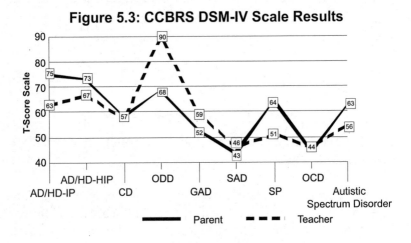

Figure 5.3: CCBRS DSM-IV Scale Results

These scales are elaborated next:

- *AD/HD – Inattentive Presentation (AD/HD-IP):* Rory's parents' rating indicates he has significant problems with concentration/sustained attention, as well as disorganisation, forgetfulness, not listening when spoken to, being distracted, lack of attention to detail, etc. His teacher's rating of inattention is slightly below the threshold.

  Using DSM-V criteria, Rory's parents note he has six of the nine inattention symptoms (with six or more symptoms indicating a significant degree of AD/HD: Inattentive Presentation); his teacher reports five of these same inattention markers.
- *AD/HD – Hyperactive–Impulsive Presentation (AD/HD-HIP):* This scale includes behaviours such as being very restless, on the go, often does not recognise danger and frequently interrupts/intrudes. With these symptoms in mind, Rory's parents and teacher both report him as having six of nine characteristics of AD/HD: Hyperactive–Impulsive Presentation.
- *Conduct Disorder (CD):* There is no significant elevation in this area, indicating the absence of conduct problems (e.g. bullying others, physical aggression and theft).
- *Oppositional Defiant Disorder (ODD):* This is clearly the highest outcome for the teacher, who reports that Rory is argumentative, angry and inclined to make negative comments about other children. On the other hand, his parents' rating indicates less of this problem in the home setting.
- *Generalised Anxiety Disorder (GAD):* The total scale score is well below threshold, indicating no concern in this area.
- *Separation Anxiety Disorder (SAD):* As with GAD, there are no concerns in this area.
- *Social Phobia (SP):* In this area, Rory's parents perceive him to have marginal problems with social connection; he tends to avoid, or is slow to warm up to, new social situations.
- *Obsessive–Compulsive Disorder (OCD):* No issues are reported here.
- *Autistic Spectrum Disorder:* The total score is below significance.

The main points that stem from both interpretations of Rory's CCBRS ratings are:

- Both his parents and teacher are most concerned about Rory's learning problems.
- There is concern about AD/HD, with his hyperactivity score meeting both empirical (elevated T-scores across raters) and DSM-V symptom criteria.
- Oppositional defiant behaviour is also elevated. However, Rory does not meet the interview-based checklist for ODD (again, using DSM-V criterion).
- No other emotional or social diagnostic category is relevant.

****

Behaviour Observations

Chapter 2 discussed behaviour observations at length and gave a number of examples. In these examples, the observation section was relatively lengthy as there was significant behaviour to record. However, in the vast majority of cases, the behaviour observation section is brief and positive, for example:

****

BEHAVIOUR OBSERVATIONS

Rory was a positive, social and cheerful participant. After an hour of testing, he became restless: squirming in his chair, making low volume sound effects, looking away from test materials, etc. However, his restlessness was momentary and he was able to refocus on the task at hand when prompted to do so.

****

Parent Interview

The types of information contained in the parent interview section of a report were discussed in Chapter 2. An example of a parent interview section of a report is:

****

PARENT INTERVIEW

Sarah and Laurence, Rory's parents, provided the following information:

- At the end of his first year in school, his teacher suggested that Rory repeat the year due to difficulty across the curriculum. He subsequently repeated junior infants.
- Rory's speech quality was poor and he was delayed in speaking. He was referred to the HSE Speech and Language Therapy Department where he received speech and language support until second class (at which point he was discharged from the service).
- In the first few years of primary school, Rory was occasionally aggressive towards peers – biting, pushing, kicking, etc. He is now less aggressive but still finds it difficult to concentrate and finish tasks.
- At home, Rory finds it very difficult to complete his homework. He is easily distracted and irritable whenever engaged in tasks that require sustained mental effort (e.g. reading and writing). His focus is slightly better for maths. Health is without issue. Sleep and diet are within normal limits.
- He relates well with his siblings; he has one older brother and one younger sister.
- He is said to relate well with children outside of school (e.g. at sports training).
- Rory's class teacher has mentioned to his parents:

  o In class, in the middle of a lesson, Rory often leaves his seat and starts talking to other children.

o   In the absence of one-to-one instruction, he is easily distracted.

o   He is popular and relates well with his classmates.

o   His problems with concentration are more noticeable when completing English and Irish lessons compared to maths; he enjoys maths assignments and his focus is better when engaged in numeracy work.

o   Some fine motor coordination difficulties are noted, particularly poor handwriting and difficulty with some aspects of daily living (e.g. buttons/zippers).

****

Teacher Interview

This section is optional, depending on whether the psychologist meets or speaks with the child's class teacher. A teacher interview (or report) is more relevant for primary school children than for older students. Obviously, in secondary school, it is not possible to interview all teachers. In some cases, the psychologist might have contact with the secondary school teacher organising the referral (e.g. a guidance counsellor, special needs coordinator, principal or year head).

If direct communication does not occur, then a report from the school might be provided instead. Obviously, parents have school reports and this type of information can be summarised in the review of records section.

An example teacher interview would be:

****

TEACHER INTERVIEW

Phone contact was made with Rory's class teacher, who observed the following:

•   Rory is frequently off-task in the classroom – swinging in his chair, looking at other children, making faces, gesturing, talking, etc. He is often involved in the affairs of other children, even though the particular event has nothing to do with him.

- He frequently interrupts during instruction.
- He is very active, sometimes jumping out of his chair for no reason. He occasionally laughs for no apparent cause.
- His behaviour is far better in small group instruction (e.g. learning support).
- He has difficulties with specific aspects of the curriculum, including oral expression, vocabulary reading, spelling and writing.
- A relative strength is maths.

****

Review of Records

'Records' refers to a variety of documents – previous professional reports, school reports, narrative written reports from teachers, school test results, referral forms, medical reports, and so on. Whatever documents parents provide, these will be summarised (if relevant) in the final report. An example review of records is provided next:

****

REVIEW OF RECORDS

The parents provided three reports, as noted below:

- In second class, Rory was assessed by a speech and language therapist. His Clinical Evaluation of Language Fundamentals (fourth edition) (CELF-4) scores were all in the 'average' band. No speech and language problems were observed and he was discharged from the HSE speech and language service.
- Also, in first class, Rory was assessed by an occupational therapist. His assessment indicated motor function within normal limits.
- The school report indicates that Rory attends learning support where the focus is on reading, listening, auditory memory,

spelling and writing, and he has the use of assistive technology, such as spelling software.

****

Summary and Analysis

After all of the sections are completed, the information is summarised and conclusions formed. In assessments, the objective is to formulate an educational diagnosis. In some cases, the outcomes are straight-forward and the diagnosis of a particular problem fits clearly with the standardised test results, parent report and behaviour observations. For example, the parents might report that their child is having dif-ficulty across the curriculum. Observations reveal similar problems with a variety of tests during the assessment. And, if the child's cog-nitive profile is uniformly low, then it is reasonably obvious that the child has general learning disability.

In other cases, the data sources do not agree and/or the test out-comes are not revealing. In these cases, it is incumbent on the assessing psychologist to make sense of disparate data and form reasonable con-clusions. What one wants to avoid are vague conclusions (e.g. 'Rory is a complex child with many needs …').

Below are three examples of summary and comment sections. In the first case, Rory's outcomes are analysed and are fairly consistent in revealing one type of learning disability and one type of emotional/ behavioural disorder. In the other two cases, the conclusions either rule out certain problems or are more tentative.

****

SUMMARY AND COMMENT

Cognitive Profile

Across various definitions of dyslexia (Department of Education and Science circulars, or definitions by advocacy organisations (e.g. Dis-ability Access Route to Education, Dyslexia Association of Ireland)), one can distil two main criteria for dyslexia:

- *General cognitive ability in, or above, the 'average' band –* General cognitive ability is the WISC-IV Full Scale Score (or General Ability Index) and the 'average' band is a standard score between 90 and 110. Rory meets this criterion as his WISC-IV Full Scale Score is 92.
- *Attainment in literacy 'below average'* – The literacy attainment tests are the WIAT-II word reading, reading speed, reading comprehension, spelling and written expression scores. Rory meets this criterion as all of his literacy attainment tests are well below a standard score of 90, with a score range of 70 to 80.

Rory also meets ancillary score patterns found in samples of children with a specific learning disability (dyslexia), uneven attainment, or predictable variation in WIAT-II scores, namely:

- *WIAT-II numerical operations/mathematical reasoning (maths) greater than word reading and writing attainments* – Rory's WIAT-II numerical operation and mathematical reasoning scores are higher than his reading and writing attainments.

Summary of Cognitive Profile

Specific learning disability (dyslexia):

- Degree: Very significant/severe
- Area(s) most impacted: All major reading variables (word reading accuracy, reading speed and reading comprehension) are 'well below average'. As for writing, both spelling and written expression are also 'well below average'.

Social–Emotional–Behavioural Profile

A second reason for this assessment was determining Rory's social–emotional–behavioural profile. The unanimous perception across raters is a marginal degree of attention deficit/hyperactivity disorder (AD/HD) – combined presentation. AD/HD was clearly manifest on the CCBRS and therefore evidenced across people and environments (including some of Rory's behaviour during the assessment). Likewise, his behaviour in the classroom can be oppositional as noted by the extremely elevated teacher score on the ODD scale.

Summary of Social–Emotional–Behaviour Profile

Attention deficit/hyperactivity disorder – combined presentation:

- There appears to be a relationship between inattention, distractibility and oppositional behaviour and particular curriculum activities. That is, Rory is most distracted and difficult to manage when learning involves language learning, such as reading and writing assignments. However, his behaviour is more focused and on-task when completing maths work. Therefore, his specific learning disability may explain some elements of his AD/HD and oppositional behaviour.

****

The next two examples of the summary and comment section are more complex. In the first case, the results of standardised testing inform us as to what is not the problem, or what does not explain the main concern (in this case, the main concern was lower language outcomes in secondary school relative to other subjects).

****

SUMMARY AND COMMENT

The chart on page two of this report shows that Jill's cognitive outcomes are consistently placed in the 'average' to 'high average' band (again refer to the 'normal' cognitive profile in Chapter 4). Thus, no formal learning problems (e.g. dyslexia) are relevant.

While Jill's language subject grades are lower than her non-language grades, uneven school achievement is not explained by a specific learning disability (dyslexia). Suggestions to address lower language outcomes are provided in the recommendations section (see Chapter 6 for a detailed discussion of the recommendations section).

****

The final example of a summary and comment section reflects both equivocal and complex outcomes:

****

SUMMARY AND COMMENT

The first reason for this assessment is to determine Tom's cognitive profile. In terms of cognitive outcomes, all of Tom's outcomes are consistently placed in, or above, the 'average' band. Thus, no formal learning problems are relevant.

A second reason for this assessment pertains to the social–emotional–behavioural spectrum. While there are consistent reports from parents and teachers of disorganisation and forgetfulness, Tom's concentration ability, as measured by a standardised test of attention span and sustained focus, is without issue. This finding shows that he can concentrate at an age-appropriate level when required to do so. While Tom's parents rate him at risk for attention deficit disorder (without hyperactivity), their report during clinical interview does not indicate significant problems with attention or frequent switching of tasks.

We also covered Asperger syndrome (AS). The necessity to further investigate AS became relevant when social detachment was touched upon. However, the parent report indicates an insignificant number of behaviours related to AS, at least using DSM-V criteria.

My diagnostic opinion is that Tom has a behaviour subset of at least three different clinical conditions, two of which are insufficient in depth or breadth to qualify as a formal diagnosis. For example, he presents with some aspects of the inattentive presentation of AD/HD (disorganisation) and some elements of AS (some social disconnection). He may also have some aspects of developmental coordination

disorder (DCD) (dyspraxia) (specific fine motor coordination problems were reported by his parents). However, a diagnosis related to
a possible coordination problem requires formal assessment by an
occupational therapist.

As Tom recently started secondary school, there is greater emphasis on organisation and social attachment, both areas of personal
weakness. In fact, some of Tom's inappropriate comments in class
could be framed as an attempt to become socially popular through
humour and attention seeking. Unfortunately, this strategy appears
to be having the reverse effect.

Summary of Cognitive and Behaviour Profile

- Cognitive profile within normal limits
- Social–emotional–behavioural profile indicates disorganisation
  but insufficient breadth of problems to indicate AD/HD (inattentive presentation)
- Insufficient depth or breadth of symptoms to indicate Asperger
  syndrome
- Some indication of coordination related problems (DCD/dysp-
  raxia), which requires a specific and specialised assessment by
  an occupational therapist

****

A Parent's View

Francis never liked school. He struggled with reading. In first
class, I asked his teacher if he might be dyslexic but was told that
he was not. He continued to dislike school and by the beginning
of third class his distress was obvious. He was upset going to bed
and seemed very unhappy and frustrated. The previous summer
he was happy and content so it seemed something was not
right. I again approached the school and Francis was assessed
by a psychologist from the National Educational Psychological
Service (NEPS). The psychologist told Francis he was dyslexic and

that he would be getting extra help in school. On the way home, after the assessment, Francis said, 'At least now I know why I am stupid.' I explained to him that he was not stupid. Within two weeks, Francis settled and was no longer upset at night. He was much happier.

He is now in third year in secondary school. He has an exemption from Irish and obtains help with his other classes during his free Irish class. While he is not a big fan of school, he is coping well.

Of particular interest in this case is the significant change in Francis' attitude towards school after the assessment. He understood that he was 'not stupid' and that there was a reason he struggled with particular aspects of the curriculum, such as reading. The improvement in his mood and the lessening of negative feelings were almost immediate.

FINAL COMMENT

Psychologists' reports will vary in length and style. However, the sections outlined in this chapter tend to be used in most reports. Perhaps the most important section of a report is the recommendation section. Here, one will find a general plan of intervention, ranging from individualising the curriculum and providing additional teaching to parenting suggestions. As the recommendations are so vital to an assessment, they are the sole focus of the next chapter.

6

Post Assessment – Recommendations

At this point in the assessment process, we should know:

- Is there a problem?
- If yes, what is the problem?
- How significant is the problem?

Once the problem has been identified, the next step is constructing a plan to address it. Herein lies the essence of the recommendation section.

Recommendations represent the psychologists' intervention methods. Psychologists develop standard packages of recommendations for a given educational diagnosis. As each case is different, some elements of the package must be altered, with new suggestions added and others deleted. The components of the packages are often the main reason why people seek (or require) an assessment. For example, a Leaving Certificate student with dyslexia will require an assessment for a number of package components, such as curriculum modifications, examination accommodations, possible assistive technology and third-level supports. Or a young primary school child with behaviour issues may need an assessment to be provided small group teaching to meet his/her needs. The implementation of the programmes recommended in a report is typically not the responsibility of the psychologist (unless they feel that they are in the best position to offer ongoing psychological support/therapy).

Perhaps the best analogy is in the medical profession. A dermatologist is an expert in assessing and diagnosing various skin maladies. The dermatologist may recommend surgery, and, at this point, refer you to a plastic or reconstructive surgeon. That is, the dermatologist conducts the assessment/diagnosis and hands over treatment to the surgeon. This is the same dynamic between the psychologist (who assesses/diagnoses) and the teacher (who provides the recommended in-class supports) and parents (who carry out the home-based plan).

What are the core elements of a recommendation section? Over time, I have found that there are essential 'domains of recommendations'. The specific recommendations will vary, depending on the age of the person and the type of outcomes. For example, reasonable accommodation for certificate examination will not be relevant to young/mid primary school children; a special needs assistant will only be recommended when certain needs are established.

The types of recommendations that are often integral to a psychologist's report are covered next.

LANGUAGE EXEMPTIONS

In the Irish educational system, children learn two languages from the outset of primary school – Irish and English. In Gaelscoileanna, the Irish language is the primary medium through which all subjects are taught, with English a mandatory subject. In non-Gaelscoileanna, English is the primary mode of instruction with Irish a mandatory subject.

Remembering the cognitive disabilities discussed in Chapter 4, a percentage of children will find the dual learning of languages extremely difficult. Take a specific learning disability, such as dyslexia. If a ten-year-old child is struggling to read words like 'weight' and 'factor', imagine how they would manage with words like 'shroich' 'pheil' and 'luath'. The phonics underlying Irish word pronunciation and spelling are very complex.

In recognition of this, the Department of Education has circulars (12/96 for primary school and 10/94 for secondary school students) which list the criteria for an exemption from the study of Irish. In relation to the types of cognitive disabilities mentioned in Chapter 4, both specific and general learning disabilities are mentioned. Although not specifically mentioned in the circular, children with specific language disabilities are at high risk of having difficulties with Irish (or any second language).

However, not all of the disabilities mentioned in Chapter 4 are logically related to language learning problems. For example, children with non-verbal learning difficulties are relatively stronger with respect to language, so learning Irish may not pose an issue for them. Likewise, there is no logical connection between emotional/behavioural disorders and the need for a language exemption. And, if a child's cognitive profile is normal, or within the average band, one cannot justify language exemptions. Therefore a language exemption is not a catch-all handed out to every child who may struggle with learning a language, but is only granted to children with specific language disabilities.

The situation is more complicated with respect to secondary school students, especially when other languages (French, German, Spanish, Japanese, etc.) are added to the mix. If students were exempted from Irish in primary school, then the exemption continues through secondary school as it does not make sense to re-introduce a subject in secondary school that was not part of the child's primary school education. With regard to other languages, there is no direct provision for an exemption from a third language, at least before the Junior Certificate cycle (this is not an issue in schools where the third language is optional). Leaving Certificate students often study three languages – English, Irish and a third language. This is because many universities require a passing grade in a third language to gain admission to courses. However, in situations where language learning is compromised, such as students who have a specific learning disability, it is possible to present with only English through the Leaving Certificate. For example, the National University of Ireland states in a document called the Psychologist's Certification Form:

> Students seeking to matriculate in the National University of Ireland are required to present six Leaving Certificate subjects, including Irish, English, and a third language. A student who is certified by a qualified professional as having a dyslexic

condition causing such a learning difficulty in relation to language acquisition as to warrant exemption may be exempted from the requirement to present Irish and/or a language other than English for matriculation. This means that the student may substitute other Leaving Certificate subjects in place of Irish and another language.

Note this form only applies to NUI colleges; non-NUI colleges have similar procedures regarding dyslexia and language exemptions and the disability access office in these schools should be contacted for clarification. Given these provisions, the timing of an assessment is vital. Obviously, a student would need to be assessed before starting their Leaving Certificate cycle. If students complete Transition Year, this would represent an ideal time for an assessment. If the student is planning on entering the Leaving Certificate cycle directly after the Junior Certificate exam, then the assessment should occur during third year.

Parents and students often ask questions about language waivers. My general response is that for young primary school children an exemption may not be necessary, even if a specific learning disability is uncovered. Why? Because cognitive profiles can change over time. If on a later re-evaluation the child's results are normal, then one may have acted prematurely. A wait-and-see approach may be more prudent. On the other hand, if a young child is severely dyslexic and the learning of Irish is proving very stressful, one can understand why an exemption may be the preferred action.

Primary school teachers who observe a child struggling with Irish will make adjustments. For example, the teacher may focus on oral Irish, reduce Irish homework and adopt a positive approach to any successful Irish learning. These interventions are extremely important and may be sufficient for the child to continue with Irish, in circumscribed form, for the remainder of primary school. Students who are dyslexic and attend a Gaelscoil cannot be logically exempted from Irish. One can recommend that the child be enrolled in a non-Gaelscoil instead (remember the story of Adrian in Chapter 1).

Parents may be reluctant to pursue an exemption because of the uncertainty of future job prospects. For example, primary and secondary teachers need a level of proficiency in Irish. Obviously, for older students who have an identified career path, and one in which Irish is not necessary, then this dilemma is removed.

For students commencing secondary school who are exempted from Irish, what should be done regarding study of a third language (French, German, Spanish, etc.)? Again, the severity of their disability is factor, such that more severe cases should probably be exempted from both languages. In less severe cases, the student could attempt the language through the Junior Certificate cycle. If difficulties with language learning continue, the student could be reviewed before starting the Leaving Certificate cycle.

Languages can be attempted at a lower level (Ordinary or Foundation level). Also, it is important to bear in mind that secondary schools may not have the resources to exempt students from more than one language. For example, a school may not have sufficient subject options for Leaving Certificate study if both languages are dropped from the student's curriculum as the student must take an alternative subject in place of the languages. Or, there may be issues with supervision and coverage for students who are formally exempted from languages. That is, these students may not have an alternative class or place to engage in supervised study. Therefore, it may be necessary for the student to remain in the language classes and engage in an alternative activity (e.g. homework in other subjects).

A typical recommendation for an exemption from Irish for a nine-year-old student would read:

****

PRIMARY SCHOOL CURRICULUM

It is recommended that Trevor be *exempted from the study of Irish* (reference to Department of Education Circular letter 12/96 point 1(c)(i)). If possible, Trevor could access learning support during his free Irish class.

****

REASONABLE ACCOMMODATION FOR CERTIFICATE EXAMINATION (RACE)

The National Educational Psychological Service (NEPS) has regularly updated documents for psychologists to determine what types of accommodations are available for students sitting the Junior and Leaving Certificate exams. The first proviso is that the State Examination Commission (SEC) is the governing body with the final determination as to whether a given accommodation is sanctioned. Psychologists can make recommendations but this does not necessarily guarantee that a specific accommodation will be accepted. The other obvious stipulation is that the accommodations apply mainly to specific learning disability (e.g. dyslexia). Clearly, across all subjects (some more so than others) there is a heavy literacy demand – students must be able to accurately and quickly read exam questions and provide written responses. Hence, students with dyslexia may be at risk of failure, since their performance is measured in their area of greatest weakness. This is not to say that other disabilities (e.g. emotional/behavioural problems and autistic spectrum disorders) are not given accommodation. In some cases, recommendations can be made for a 'special centre', essentially a separate examination room for students with low incidence disabilities. Obviously, the assessing psychologist must justify why a special centre is requested given the particular disability and how it will manifest in exam conditions.

In some of the more common exam arrangements (e.g. a reader (someone who reads the questions to the student) and/or spelling waiver), it is not required that general cognitive ability be measured. That is, if a student's word reading and spelling measure are low, this may be sufficient to warrant an accommodation (provided that additional support – writing samples, reading speeds, reading accuracy in context, school grades, etc. – are also supportive of said accommodation). In the absence of knowing general ability, school attainment may be low due to a general learning difficulty (and not those more specific in nature). In other words, students with general learning difficulties can also be considered for exam accommodations. Students with a motor disability, such as dyspraxia, may also be considered for exam accommodations. If handwriting is an issue, alternative response formats (e.g. taped dictation or use of a computer or scribe) can be recommended.

Below is an example of a report written for a Leaving Certificate student using the 2013 RACE guidelines (explanations are in parentheses).

****

REASONABLE ACCOMMODATION FOR CERTIFICATE EXAMINATION

With regard to eligibility for a *reader*, the Guidelines for Psychologists in the 2013 RACE document require the following:

- *Indication of SLD (specific learning disability):* Josephine meets this criterion as noted in the preceding section (the summary and comment or conclusion section will detail why SLD is evident).
- *Standard scores of less than 85 on reading tests:* Josephine easily meets this criterion as her word reading standard score was 53 (the word reading test is normally the WIAT-II word reading measure).
- *Evidence of difficulty reading connected text*, as manifest through (a) reading rates below 90 words per minute (wpm) or (b) a reading error rate greater than 7 per cent: Josephine meets both requirements: (a) some of her reading rates were below 90 wpm and (b) her error rate on orally read material was 36 per cent (WIAT-II reading comprehension oral reading samples).

As Josephine meets all criteria, an exam reader is strongly recommended.

There are three qualifying criteria for a *spelling waiver*. The specific criteria and Josephine's position in regard to each eligibility marker is outlined next:

- *Indication of SLD*: Same as for reader.
- *Standard scores of less than 85 on spelling tests*: Josephine clearly meets this criterion as her word spelling standard score was 58.

- *Spelling/punctuation/grammar error rate of 8 per cent or greater*: Josephine meets this criterion as her cumulative errors for SPG was 29 per cent of the total word count (see Appendix 1 – in this appendix, the student's writing sample is provided, as in the sample report provided in Chapter 1. The SPG errors are counted and a percentage is obtained from the ratio of errors to total word count).

Therefore, it is strongly recommended that Josephine be granted a *waiver for spelling, grammar and punctuation/capitalisation* for the *English* and *Irish* papers (spelling waivers only apply to languages so these were the two languages Josephine was planning to sit for her Leaving Certificate).

Regarding the use of a *scribe* (an individual who reads aloud the questions and writes the student's oral response to the question) for state examination, the following criteria are provided in the 2013 RACE Guidelines:

- *Indication of SLD*: Same as for reader/spelling waiver.
- Scripts are deemed 'unintelligible' if the *spelling/punctuation/grammar error rate is 20 per cent or greater*. Josephine meets this criteria as her cumulative errors for SPG were 29 per cent of the total word count (see Appendix 1).

An additional point relevant to being granted a scribe:

- *WISC-IV verbal comprehension score within the 'average' band*: this implies that Josephine's exam performance will be enhanced when presenting her exam answers in oral rather than written form.

Therefore, it is strongly recommended that *Josephine be granted a scribe* for examinations in which long essay responses are required. If possible, Josephine should use a scribe for upcoming (and future) end-of-term exams.

****

RESOURCE SUPPORT

Firstly, we need to clarify the difference between resource and learning support. Learning support is conducted in small groups by a specially designated teacher, with the focus on academic skills. Learning support can be divided into English and Maths support. On the other hand, resource teaching is typically one-to-one and is more specialised in focus, including behaviour, social, emotional, language, motor coordination and assistive technology support.

Learning support does not require a psychoeducational evaluation. Students in primary school can be provided learning support based on school observations/tests. If problems are identified, the school can suggest that the child receive support in the form of extra teaching in their area of need (e.g. reading and/or maths). Support is usually provided in a group context and may be pull-out (the child leaves their classroom to go to another room for small group teaching) or provided through separate small group teaching in the home room (the main room where all children are instructed for the majority of the school day).

Many of the children who obtain learning support likely have one of the cognitive disabilities mentioned in Chapter 4, notably specific, general or comprehension disabilities. All of the cognitive disabilities are considered 'high incidence' problems and, therefore, can be managed without external assessment. As a result, these disabilities may not be formally detected unless parents/teachers desire an assessment. Typically, these assessments occur at any point in primary school with the referral based on lack of progress, desire of the referring teacher to learn of teaching methods based on the child's cognitive strengths/weaknesses, and/or a child struggling with specific aspects of curriculum (e.g. Irish).

Resource support, on the other hand, requires specialised and external assessment. All problems which are not cognitive disabilities (all other categories in Chapter 4: physical/medical conditions, emotional/behavioural/autistic spectrum, and speech/language and motor problems) are 'low incidence' disabilities and may be entitled to resource support. Additional professional assessments that are required for allocating resource hours may need to come from psychologists, psychiatrists, speech and language therapists, occupational therapists and medical consultants.

Low incidence disabilities are allocated specific hours. For example, children with AD/HD (considered an emotional/behavioural disorder) receive three-and-a-half hours of weekly support; students with specific speech and language disorder are granted four hours per week. Children with autistic spectrum disorders are allocated five hours of resource teaching per week (the maximum).

If resource hours are granted, these hours are not necessarily deployed on a one-to-one basis. The allocation means that the child will receive the given teaching hours, but these hours may be group and/or individual teaching. The size of the resource group depends on how many children are already allocated hours for a given resource teacher. Also, the resource teacher may have to balance a schedule between different schools.

A psychologist can recommend one-to-one support, but, like many other recommendations, this may not occur given administrative constraints (e.g. caseloads, schedules and number of schools served by the resource teacher). Ideally, the psychologist will recommend areas of high priority and methods to teach/manage behaviour.

A sample of a resource recommendation is provided next.

****

RESOURCE SUPPORT

Eamon is eligible for four hours of weekly resource support as he meets all criteria for a specific speech and language disorder. Consider the following areas in the provision of support:

Language Comprehension

• Use 'paired language' where natural conversation is the focus. Follow Eamon's interests and hobbies, as well as discussing Eamon's daily experiences. However, do not ask too many questions. The conversation should be interactive, not interrogational.

- Pause and wait – allow silence so Eamon can construct his thoughts.
- During paired language, if Eamon uses incorrect grammar (e.g. 'I done my homework'), do not correct him, but repeat the sentence in a correct form ('I did my homework').
- Ask Eamon to provide words for collections of similar objects, e.g. 'What word do we use for things we wear?', 'What word do we use for things we eat with?'
- Ask Eamon to classify/group objects: 'How are a thimble, needle, thread and scissors alike?'
- Focus on similarities and differences. For example, list commonalities between a boat and a train and also identify the unique aspects of these modes of transport.
- Compile a picture dictionary. For example, use magazines and cut out pictures of boats and trains.
- During conversation, identify specific words that may have multiple meanings (e.g. 'wear'). Have Eamon use a dictionary to look up the word and write brief definitions of the different uses of the word.
- Listen to books on tape and retell the story in sequence. Ask Eamon what characters might be feeling and thinking. Ask him to think of different story endings.
- Use Cloze (fill-in-the-blank) procedures to develop syntactic awareness (e.g. 'The _____ sings in the tree').
- Give Eamon jumbled sentences and ask him to write/say/arrange word cards in the correct order.
- Have Eamon listen to, and follow, verbal instructions (e.g. 'Draw a circle with two dots inside it and a cross underneath it').
- Discuss current events and talk about notions of fairness, law, politics, morality, etc. Have Eamon report on newspaper/magazine articles.
- Play word games (e.g. Scrabble, Pictionary and Trivial Pursuit). Use show-and-tell games.
- Use areas of interest. For example, if Eamon is interested in sports, ask about how the game is played, how competitions are organised, to explain transfer of players and management,

etc. The idea is allow Eamon to express ideas in an area of high interest.

- Discuss social etiquette, rules and standards (e.g. 'What should you do if another child tells a story about you that is not true?', 'Why do we pay for our rubbish to be collected?').
- Along these lines, consider divergent thinking activities (e.g. 'Why do many foods need to be cooked?'). Have Eamon think of as many reasons as he can.
- Stimulate and encourage everyday reasoning and thinking in natural contexts (e.g. 'What do you do when you start a class-room writing assignment but can't find something to write with in your bag?').
- Discuss problem situations using current events/world situations.
- Focus on 'why' and 'how' questions (e.g. 'How does satellite television work?', 'Why is it important for people to pay taxes?').
- Use verbal comprehension software such as mind-mapping software or Kidspiration (a type of mind-mapping software program which helps children understand the relationships between concepts).
- Ensure Eamon has constant access to a pocket dictionary and thesaurus.
- Analyse prefixes and suffixes (e.g. 'un', 'dis', 'less' and 'ly').
- Pick five to ten words a week. These words should be of interest to Eamon (related to activities he enjoys, hobbies, etc.). The words can be of any level of complexity. Ask Eamon to look up the words in a dictionary and write a brief definition, or use one or two synonyms. Keep a list and make this Eamon's personal dictionary.
- Teach and review the meaning of synonym and antonym. Give examples and have Eamon develop a personal dictionary.
- Have Eamon use a computer with a standard word processor. Show him how to use the thesaurus on the word processor.
- Expose Eamon to stimulating experiences (e.g. a museum) and have him keep a journal.
- Do child-friendly crossword puzzles and ask Eamon to look up definitions of new words or words he does not know the meaning of.

Auditory Memory

- Following directions – present a short series of discrete verbal requests such as:

  o Place three objects in front of Eamon and say, 'Let's play a memory game with these things. Put the green block into the container, put the red Lego piece on the Lego board, and place the teddy bear under the bed.' Increase the number of objects as Eamon's span of immediate memory increases.

  o Give Eamon colouring pens and paper and have him follow a series of verbal directions, e.g. 'Draw a big red square, put a green circle underneath the square, and draw a black line from the middle of the circle to the upper right-hand corner of the square.'

- Repeating information – ask Eamon to immediately repeat numbers, words, sentences and rhythms:

  o Give a series of numbers, such as, '6, 3, 5, 4, 9.' Ask Eamon to immediately repeat them. Ask questions and give instructions about the numbers such as, 'Write the fourth number', 'What is the smallest/largest number?' and 'What number is closest to your age?'

  o Provide a list of words, like, 'pen, ball, car, book', and have Eamon immediately repeat the list. Ask him to repeat a particular word position (e.g. 'What was the second word?'). Increase the length of the list as he improves.

  o Ask Eamon to repeat a sentence like, 'The dog bit the big boy on the leg.' Increase sentence length and word complexity as needed.

  o Tap out or clap a rhythm and have him repeat it.

  o Recite poems, songs and sayings.

- Listen for detail: Use the number or letter line and say, '1, 2, 3 (pause – child supplies missing item), 5, 6, 7 (pause – child supplies missing item), 9, etc.'

- Play listening games, e.g. 'I went to the moon and took my space-suit.' Eamon repeats sentence and adds another item: 'I went to the moon and took my spacesuit and my bike.' Add another item, then Eamon does the same, etc.
- Read/tell stories: After reading or telling a short story, have Eamon retell the story, mentioning each event in order (exact word recall is not important, just the major details/events). Ask Eamon questions about the story (e.g. who, what, when, where, how).
- Teach Eamon memory strategies. For example, teach him to group items (break a five-digit number into one group of three numbers, and one of two numbers). Or, group words in a list (e.g. school supplies – pen, book, ruler; and toys – ball, car, doll).
- Use auditory memory software (such as Memory Booster).

Maths

- Analyse Eamon's maths skills based on the developmental nature of maths instruction:

  o Infants – maths readiness skills, such as counting, sets, matching, classification and writing numbers
  o First and second class – computation of addition and subtraction with one- and two-digit numbers
  o Third class – multiplication facts, regrouping for adding and subtracting, fraction concepts
  o Fourth class – division facts and extended use of all basic operations
  o Fifth class – fractions, decimals, long division and mixed numbers
  o Sixth class – percentages, three-/four-place multipliers, etc.

- Also, consider the division between pure computation (8 + 6 = ?) and word problems: 'John has eight marbles. He bought six more. How many marbles does he now have altogether?' If the child is significantly better in computation skill then their reasoning and/or reading skills may be suspect.

- Specify exactly the nature of the problem (e.g. difficulty with borrowing during two- and three-digit subtraction).
- Check to see if errors may be due to carelessness (e.g. $8 - 6 = 14$ (the child adds when he should subtract)).
- Use concrete teaching materials (e.g. for simple addition, use objects so the child can visually see that $5 + 3 = 8$).
- Maths computation skill is largely a function of drill and practice. Therefore, make sure Eamon practises his maths skills on a daily basis.
- Model and demonstrate skill (e.g. how to subtract 19 from 34).
- Make the connection clear between number skill and many everyday living tasks, such as keeping time, determining the rules of a competition (e.g. which team wins on aggregate), money, measuring, etc.
- Show Eamon how maths is related to solving problems through reasoning and numbers. The scientific method is based on numbers and children should be given easy-to-do experiments which involve reasoning, collecting information (numbers) and then doing sums.
- Use programmed teaching materials which sequence maths problems. Use structured modules so when the child demonstrates a specific skill (e.g. 8 out of 10 correct answers), move to the next unit, etc.
- Use computer software to help develop maths skills (e.g. Numbershark).
- Emphasise key words in age-expected problems (e.g. point to the *third* bowl from the dog, *cover* three birds with your hand, which tank has *more* fish?).
- Have Eamon visualise and draw out word problems. For example, consider the problem below:

'Robert has 4 stones. Together Robert and Max have 12 stones. How many stones does Max have?'

Encourage Eamon to picture 12 stones, with 4 belonging to Robert. He could draw 12 stones and circle 4 of them, and then count the remainder.

Visual Learner

Use Eamon's visual–spatial strength in the teaching process. Eamon fits the criteria of being a visual learner. A visual learner (in contrast to the auditory learner described in Chapter 4) is someone who:

- Recalls information better when it is seen rather than heard
- Is visually perceptive (notices changes in the environment)
- Has good visual discrimination skill (e.g. can perceive likeness and differences in letter shapes)
- May ignore verbal directions and daydream during classes that are predominately verbal
- Has difficulty discriminating between orally presented sounds (e.g. 'pin' versus 'pen')
- Uses gestures instead of words and has a smaller vocabulary compared with peers
- Has difficulty with sound blending and learning from phonics

General Teaching Tips for Visual Learners

- Emphasise visual cues and give as little auditory input as possible.
- Assess word knowledge and start at Eamon's level. Present new information visually.
- Auditory input should be brief and to the point. Avoid complex oral directions.
- Use visual instruction methods as often as possible (e.g. charts, overhead projections and movies).
- Speak clearly and slowly. Always face Eamon when speaking. Use gestures when speaking.
- Maintain a quiet room and sit Eamon close to you during group instruction.
- Write out instructions for Eamon. Teach him to make lists.

Reading Methods for a Visual Learner

Use patterned reading. Patterned reading is an approach that emphasises letter patterns in words.

- Emphasise word families (BALL → CALL, FALL, HALL, MALL, TALL, WALL).
- Divide word syllables with marks like /.
- Always have words clearly printed on large index cards.
- Keep a list of words with the same prefixes (e.g. un-, mis-) and suffixes (e.g. -tion, -ance, -edge).
- Keep a list of verbs in different forms: COMPLETE → COMPLETES, COMPLETED, COMPLETING, COMPLETELY, COMPLETION.
- Have Eamon keep a file of frequently mispronounced words.
- Use computer-assisted reading programs such as Texthelp, Read & Write Gold or Lexia. Computer methods can take full advantage of the visual elements of letter patterns, as some of the programs have toolbars which break words into parts, group words according to patterns, and so on.
- Use a structured visually based reading programme which requires writing and completing exercises (e.g. Alpha to Omega).
- Phonics should be not used until Eamon has a reasonably large reading vocabulary. Then phonics can be introduced gradually and with reference to high-frequency words Eamon already knows. Patterned analysis methods (which emphasise visually similar letter patterns) can be used in conjunction with phonics at this point.

General Teaching Suggestions

Based on observations of Eamon during the assessment, consider the following as key elements in the teaching process:

- Allow Eamon considerable wait time to solve problems and answer oral/written questions. In the context of his assessment, he was provided ample time to deliberate and was not hurried or pressed for responses. Only after it was clear that he was unable to respond was he prompted or it was assumed that a response was not forthcoming.

- During the wait time period, be patient and do not ask questions or provide hints or suggestions on how to solve the problem. The actual wait period can vary but should probably not exceed 30 seconds.
- Praise is vital for any partially correct use of a procedure (e.g. borrowing when subtracting).

Assistive Technology

(covered later in this chapter)

****

SPECIAL NEEDS ASSISTANT

As set out in DES Circular 07/02, 'Special Needs Assistants (SNA) are recruited specifically to assist in the *care* of pupils with disabilities in an educational context' (my emphasis). Students with care needs require the type of assistance that goes well beyond the purview of existing teaching staff. Some examples of care needs:

- Movement-related assistance for a student with a significant visual impairment
- Assistance with toileting for a student with a physical handicap. This same student may also need assistance with his/her bag, such as locating and moving books, and organising and finding necessary learning materials. Assistance also may be required during lunch breaks.
- Specialised assistance and supervision in the school yard for a student with a behavioural disorder who may be a danger to others (e.g. who throws objects at students or displays aggression towards other members of the class), as this type of one-to-one monitoring could not be undertaken by a supervising class teacher

The role of an SNA is of a non-teaching nature, such as:

- Assisting children with self-help needs (e.g. clothing, feeding, hygiene, use of the toilet and movement)
- Helping children with physical/movement disabilities manage learning materials and complete independent work at their desk
- Supervision and monitoring of activities outside of class (on the school yard, on field trips, assisting with movement into and out of school, etc.)
- Helping with transitions from class to other areas of school

An example of a recommendation for an SNA follows.

****

Special Needs Assistant (SNA) (Full-Time)

In reviewing relevant circulars in this area, and especially criteria used by the National Council for Special Education (NCSE) to deter-mine the level of resources for a school, the key issue is, 'Are there care or safety needs arising from the diagnosis?' One of the care/safety needs relevant to AD/HD (the primary diagnosis in this case; general learning disability was the cognitive disability) is 'behaviour is such that pupils are a danger to themselves or other pupils.'

In Zachary's case, he is very aggressive to other children in school – biting, pinching, kicking, pushing, etc. Thus, Zachary represents a danger to other children and this is one rationale for a special needs assistant. Other SNA rationales are:

- Breaks and lunch – assisting in tidying up his desk
- Assist with organisation of school materials – books, folders, paper/pencils and other task-relevant material
- Management of Zachery's inattention and over-activity during class (to reduce the disruptive nature of this behaviour for other students)
- The same degree of supervision would be required for out-of-school activities, assemblies, dispersal periods, etc.

- There are no care needs regarding physical disability/toilet use, etc.
- Monitoring social exclusion and concurrently facilitating social interaction. Given aggression to other children, Zachary is at risk of being excluded during play and class activities. An SNA could manage and encourage social interaction.
- Setting up a clear visual schedule (e.g. a chart taped to his desk) with a daily calendar of events. The SNA would review each task.
- Monitoring learning and understanding as Zachary is very likely to be confused about task instructions
- Coordinating regular movement breaks (e.g. a walk outside) at pre-determined intervals

****

HOME TUITION

The primary reason for home-based tuition is significant school absence due to long-term chronic medical conditions. In some cases, a child may not be able to attend school due to illness. In other cases, students with certain forms of autistic spectrum disorder may not be able to cope with the social interaction demands of school; these same students may also find transitions extremely difficult and may became very distressed when school routine is disturbed (e.g. if a teacher needs to momentarily leave the room this can lead to feelings of panic and anxiety).

A recommendation for home schooling is provided below.

****

HOME SCHOOLING/TUITION

Rosemary meets DSM-V criteria for an autistic disorder spectrum. It is clear from the parent and teacher reports that Rosemary is unable to cope with the social and sometimes variable environment typical of secondary school. She has significant difficulty dealing with the daily interactional and communication expectations of a mainstream secondary school. To cope, she began to leave school during the day and was starting to self-harm. Therefore, home schooling is recommended for the duration of secondary school.

An initial contact was made with the Home Tuition division of the Special Education Section of the Department of Education and Skills in Athlone. When this report is received, it is also strongly recommended that it be provided to the school liaison officer.

****

SPECIAL UNITS

There are mainstream schools with special units, which are specialised classrooms employing small group instruction for a specific categorical need (e.g. autistic spectrum disorders, dyslexia and language disorders). In the case of dyslexia, the class may be called a 'reading unit'. These specialised classrooms offer a mixture of small group instruction and integration with the mainstream class group for specific activities. The teachers associated with these units are typically specialised in the teaching of the particular group.

To access special units, a specific application is required with relevant reports. Usually, there are deadlines for the applications and the particular unit will probably have criteria for admission. A recommendation for a reading unit is provided below.

****

ST MARY'S SCHOOL READING UNIT

Despite participating in the Reading Recovery programme, Anne obtained very low reading/spelling scores. Her spelling has not progressed beyond consonant–vowel–consonant (cvc) words, and a small percentage of four-letter words. She has an extremely limited automatic reading vocabulary and must resort to slow and laborious 'sounding out' to decode numerous words which should already be in her reading range.

Therefore, a more intensive immersion programme is recommended, such as the St Mary's School Reading Unit. While I am unaware of the criteria for admission, the chart on page X of this report should assist the selection committee. Also, Anne does not present with behaviour or social issues, so she is categorically dyslexic and all other special educational needs have been ruled out.

Within an intensive reading unit, the focus would naturally be:

Reading

- Focus on oral reading of materials in Anne's instructional reading level (roughly two years below her current age).
- Allow her time to inspect and deliberate before attempting words which are not immediately familiar. When she does successfully sound out a word, praise enthusiastically.
- Use a structured phonics programme (e.g. Alpha to Omega, Orton–Gillingham products, Phono-Graphix or GRASP).

Language Experience Approach

Reading is viewed as an extension of language arts. Reading is interdependent on the development of listening, speaking and writing skills. The raw materials are the experiences and language of the child. Essentially, the child begins by dictating a story to the teacher. The story is written down by the teacher and becomes the materials the child will read. The logic is:

- What I can think about, I can talk about.
- What I can say, I can write (or someone can write for me).
- What I can write, I can read.
- I can read what others write for me.

Language Experience Procedure

- Tell the student you would like her to dictate a story to you so you will have something to read about. Talk about areas of interest. Decide on a title (e.g. *Roses*). Print the title large and clear, point to it and ask the child to read the title to you. Then the child dictates a story to you, e.g. 'My mummy planted roses in our garden.' Print each word large and clearly. Use the exact language of the student. Make sure the student watches you as you write each word of the story. Say each word as you write it and point to it with your finger. Stop after each sentence and have the student say each word and point to it. Do this after each sentence. After finishing, read the entire story aloud, pointing to each word as you read it. Then have the student do likewise. Quickly call miscues to the student's attention and continue.

- The story length will vary according to the learner's needs. After it is finished, type it up and have the student read it at your next meeting. If she does this without error, reward and praise her appropriately and create a new story. After a number of stories, bind them and let the student illustrate the cover.

- For beginning readers or readers with severe reading problems, take words from the story to develop a list of a high-frequency words. Always provide visual associations for child on cards. For example:

Rose

- After around 20–50 frequently occurring words are learned, begin to teach word families based on them.

Multi-Sensory Method

The following procedure uses multiple sensory modalities – visual, auditory, kinaesthetic and tactile – to facilitate automatic, fluent reading.

- Make a box for a word file. Cut out words from poster board or heavy card stock.

- Allow the child to select a few unknown words from a story you have read aloud.
- Write a word the child selected on the poster board card with heavy crayons (to create texture) either in block letters or in cursive script.
- The child traces this word using the index finger on the hand used for writing. While tracing, the child says the word aloud. This process is repeated until the child can write the word without looking at it. The child should say the word as it is actually pronounced. Do not let the child sound out each individual letter.
- The child writes the word three times on three separate pieces of paper, without looking at the original card. *Do not allow the child to look back and forth between the copy and the original work*. If an error is made, start again on new paper rather than correcting the error.
- File word cards alphabetically. Begin by using only the first letter of the word, and then move toward full alphabetisation.
- Practice words daily until they are 100 per cent correct for ten consecutive days.

Spelling/Written Expression

Cued Spelling

1. SPELLER CHOOSES WORD
Speller chooses high-interest words regardless of complexity.

2. CHECK RIGHT SPELLING AND PUT IN DIARY
Check spelling of word in dictionary, and put a master version in cued spelling diary.

3. READ THE WORD – TOGETHER AND ALONE
Pair read word together, then child reads word alone. Child must be able to pronounce word before spelling it.

4. CHOOSE CUES
Child chooses cues (prompts, reminders) to enable recall of the written structure of the word. A list of possible cues is:

- Rules (e.g. 'i before e except after c')
- Words in words (e.g. 'care/less' 'water/fall')
- Fronts/backs (fronts like 'un-' and 'pre-' and backs like '-ght', '-ance' and '-ate')
- Families (e.g. '-ent' family – bent, cent, dent, gent, pent, vent)
- Images/pictures of words (e.g. remember Wednesday by thinking of people getting wed on Wednesday)
- Shrink a word by condensing it to a single embedded word in the middle (e.g. 'separate' by thinking of 'par' in the middle). Then add the beginning and ending letters from this shrunken word: 'se' and 'ate'.
- Grow words like n e c e s s a r y (1 collar and 2 socks). The idea is to reduce the most likely spelling error with a mnemonic – the one collar refers to one 'c' and the two socks refers to two 's's – and then grow the word around this key point. So, the speller can simply add 'ne', 'e' and 'ary' around the collar and socks.
- Use mnemonics, as mentioned above, but as isolated cues. For example, 'there is plenty of room in accommodation for two "c"s and two "m"s.'
- Fix meaning (spelling is enhanced if the child knows the exact meaning of a word; discuss word meaning until it is fixed in the child's mind)
- Jokes/funnies (silly and comic things)

The helper can discuss all of these with the child, but the child selects the cues to use. They must be meaningful to the child.

5. SAY CUES TOGETHER
Both adult and child say cues aloud simultaneously.

6. CHILD SAYS CUE, HELPER WRITES WORD

Child says cues out loud while adult writes dictated word on scrap paper. Adult models required behaviour. Adult covers previous tries.

7. HELPER SAYS CUE. CHILD WRITES WORD

Child checks spelling. Praise her if she self-corrects misspelling before checking master. Only if the child is unable to check word does the helper intervene.

8. CHILD SAYS CUE AND WRITES WORD

If correct, continue to step 9. If incorrect, encourage the child to cross out misspelling immediately to delete incorrect form from mind. Return to step 7.

9. CHILD WRITES WORD FAST

Child writes word quickly. Cues may or may not be used, or used sub-vocally. Helper praises child if word is correctly spelled.

10. CHILD READS WORD

To remind child of wholeness of word and associated meaning

After each session, have a speed review:
The helper dictates all the words learned in the session in random order. The child writes the words as quickly as possible and checks spelling. Child checks with master version in diary. If any words are wrong, do steps 1–10 again.

After each week have a mastery review:
Child quickly writes down all words for the week and checks spelling. Decide what to do about wrong words – can include failed words in next week's target words.

Construct a Spelling Diary

Week of:		
Day	**Master Word List**	**Speed Review Score**
Monday		
Tuesday		
Wednesday		
Thursday		
Friday		
Saturday		
Sunday		
Master Review Score		
Comments		

Cued spelling should be done three times per week for fifteen minutes each session, with an initial trial period of six weeks.

Paired Writing

Idea

- Step 1: Choose a topic. The topic used in this example is 'My pet'.
- Step 2: Teacher asks questions about the pet such as its name, age, how did you get the pet, what does the pet eat, is it healthy, who cares for the pet, do you play with it? The teacher writes the answers given.
- Step 3: Child and teacher chose from the support stage below.

Draft

Child and teacher choose the most appropriate support stage from below:

Stage 1	Stage 2	Stage 3	Stage 4
Teacher writes all and child copies all	Teacher writes difficult words and child writes everything else	Child writes all and teacher tells child how to spell difficult words	Child writes it all

Read

Teacher reads draft out loud. Then child reads draft out loud and teacher re-reads any words the child has incorrectly pronounced.

Edit

Teacher marks where to improve:

- Meaning
- Order
- Spelling
- Punctuation

Child also edits paper. Both teacher and child suggest changes and use a dictionary to look up unfamiliar words. Child makes changes to the text.

Final copy

Child copies out text from draft. Either teacher or child may type up final text.

****

ASSISTIVE TECHNOLOGY

Some disabilities, if severe, or greatly interfering with educational progress, may require assistive technology (AT). Assistive technologies are globally classified as (a) hardware in the form of standalone equipment/devices, such as a reading pen, Livescribe pulse pen, laptop, tablet computer or printer, or (b) software (e.g. spelling programs like Wordshark, reading programs like Reading Booster, and maths programs such as Numeracy Workout). There are many available software programs. For dyslexia, there are text-to-speech programs (e.g. Read&Write Gold), where the software can act as a reader and read aloud scanned text (from book to PC) to the student. Or, vice versa, there is speech-to-text software (e.g. Dragon), where the student can train his/her voice to 'scribe' information to the computer where it is automatically typed (particularly important for students who have significant problems with written expression and/or handwriting).

Below are some examples of AT recommendations.

****

ASSISTIVE TECHNOLOGY

It is recommended that the school determines whether a NCSE technology grant for David applies given the severity of his specific learning disability (dyslexia and dyscalculia) (normal general intelligence but reading ability below a standard score of 70; David also presents with math scores below the 'average' band, although not as low as his reading outcomes). It is unlikely that David will succeed in school to the level of his general cognitive ability without the use of assistive technologies. The following assistive technologies are vital to David's effective education:

It is essential that David has his own PC to function. The PC must have hardware specifications required to run the reading/writing/maths software noted below.

- Lexia – Enables readers of all levels to improve their skills
- Reading Booster – For comprehension and vocabulary
- Wordshark – A spelling program
- Numeracy Workout (ages 7–13)
- MathsBook Plus – Very structured and easily identified 'tens' and 'units' across all basic operations

- Math Problem Solver – Consists of 300 word problems in areas of money, measurement, time, understanding charts/graphs, etc.
- Numeracy Bank series – A number of multiple choice items that can be used for teaching/testing

****

A second example of an assistive technology recommendation is provided below.

****

ASSISTIVE TECHNOLOGY (AT)

It is suggested that the school contact the local NCSE to determine the relevance of a technology grant given Colm's severe and specific learning disability (dyslexia). His writing is illegible and he cannot take notes in class (he cannot read his own notes). Clearly, Colm will not succeed in school to the level of his general cognitive ability without the use of assistive technologies. The following assistive technologies are vital to Colm's effective education:

- It is essential that Colm has his own portable PC to function. The PC must have hardware specifications required to run the writing and dictation software noted below:

  o Dragon Naturally Speaking: This is voice recognition software. Essentially, the computer acts as a scribe. A program like Dragon is the single most important AT for Colm. Given his verbal ability, he can orally dictate information and then print out his essays. This will bypass illegible handwriting and general problems with written expression.

- A separate hardware device that is essential for Colm is a Dictaphone or Livescribe pulse pen. Obviously, Colm requires a method to record class notes which does not involve traditional pencil and paper.

I understand that the NCSE would be involved in sourcing/pricing the above hardware and software. As for training, especially Dragon, this requires dedicated practice and could be the remit of learning support. The same is true with the Livescribe pulse pen.

****

DISABILITY ACCESS ROUTE TO EDUCATION (DARE)

Students with disabilities are at a disadvantage when it comes to the myriad processes fundamental to state exam performance. If a student has a short attention span then prolonged and continuous book study will not work. If a student has difficulty with the core elements of efficient reading/writing, it does not bode well for success in exams in which extensive reading and writing are the core components. Therefore, the Disability Access Route to Education (DARE) was developed to assist students with disabilities to achieve college courses on a reduced point basis. DARE is (as stated on the DARE website):

> ... for school leavers who have the ability to benefit from and succeed in higher education but who may not be able to meet the points for their preferred course due to the impact of their disability.

The DARE website lists the types of disabilities considered and the eligibility standards for each disability. The DARE website gives very specific eligibility criteria for dyslexia and dyscalculia. Regarding dyslexia, the criteria are:

- General ability (Full Scale Score, GAI) falls at or above a standard score of 90

  and

- Attainment is at or below the 10th percentile (standard score of 81 or lower) in two different literacy areas, from the following:

- o Single word reading (e.g. WIAT-II word reading)
- o Reading accuracy (where the number of words read in continuous text are counted and the raw score is converted to a standard score; the WIAT-II does not have a standard score for words read correctly in passage reading)
- o Reading comprehension (e.g. WIAT-II reading comprehension)
- o Reading speed/fluency (e.g. the WIAT-II has standard score conversion tables for reading speeds up to the age of 16 years and 11 months)
- o Pseudoword decoding (the WIAT-II has this measure, although it is not discussed at length in this book; the decision to use this particular test is up to each assessing psychologist)
- o Spelling (e.g. WIAT-II spelling)
- o Writing speed (the WIAT-II does not have a writing speed standard score; however, the DARE website lists other measures that can be considered for writing speed)
- o Written expression (e.g. WIAT-II written expression)

For dyscalculia, the first criterion is the same (full scale or general ability score at or greater than 90), while the attainment standard must be at or below the 10th percentile (standard score of 81 or lower) in two different mathematical areas:

- Mathematical reasoning (e.g. WIAT-II mathematical reasoning)
- Mathematical computation (e.g. WIAT-II numerical operations)

Looking at the cognitive profiles for dyslexia and dyscalculia discussed in Chapter 4, does your child meet the DARE criteria?

DARE is only relevant to participating colleges. There are thirteen institutions in total that participate in the DARE scheme: Athlone Institute of Technology, Cork Institute of Technology, Dublin City University, Dublin Institute of Technology, Mater Dei Institute of Education, Maynooth University, National College of Ireland, NUI Galway, Pontifical University Maynooth, Trinity College Dublin, University College Cork, University College Dublin and University of

Limerick. Each college has a designated DARE representative and this person can be contacted to learn more about DARE.

A recommendation regarding DARE follows.

****

A RECOMMENDATION FOR DARE

Barbara meets the Disability Access Route to Education (DARE) criteria for a specific learning disability (dyslexia). Her Wechsler Adult Intelligence Scale (fourth edition) (WAIS-IV) General Ability Index (GAI) score of 92 is above the cut-off score of 90. She also has two different literacy domain standard scores below the 10th percentile (standard score of 81) – on the WIAT-II reading comprehension and written expression tests. WIAT-II reading comprehension and written expression represent different literacy domains, as noted on the DARE website.

However, DARE may not be applicable to Barbara as her choice of third-level CAO college is not listed as participating in the DARE scheme.

****

FURTHER ASSESSMENT

Psychologists are not always one-stop shops. The cognitive profiles may stand alone, or may suggest the need for further assessment by other specialists (e.g. occupational therapists, speech and language therapists or child psychiatrists). As mentioned previously, some educational disabilities require several assessments (e.g. dyspraxia and specific speech and language disorder).

One is never sure what might emerge from an assessment. Occasionally, the results indicate problems that may not have been previously considered (or dismissed as not significant issues). In situations where further assessment is required, the assessing psychologist will make a recommendation for another professional assessment. As an example, consider the recommendation below.

****

RECOMMENDATION FOR FURTHER ASSESSMENT

Consider an occupational therapist (OT) assessment with respect to dyspraxia. An OT evaluation is required to fully investigate concerns about motor functions. The assessing OT will used standardised tests and other sources of data to determine gross and fine motor function. Contact [name] at [number].

****

RECOMMENDATIONS FOR PARENTS

Psychologist's reports usually have a section dedicated solely to parent implementation. These recommendations will vary considerably, depending on the reason for the assessment and the outcomes. The general spirit of this section is that parents can undertake certain strategies (e.g. reading methods with their child, behaviour management) that may be useful and that do not require any further or specialised training. Many parents may have tried some of these strategies already and have not found them particularly successful. If these topics are given time during the parent interview, the assessing psychologist might be able to suggest a different approach or identify problems in the implementation of previous strategies.

What follows are two different sets of parental recommendations based on different assessments. The first case involves a clear finding of dyslexia and the parent recommendations concern strategies to deal with dyslexia. The second case involves a child whose behaviour is an issue. But firstly, recommendations for parents of a child with dyslexia:

****

IDEAS AND HANDOUTS FOR PARENTS OF A DYSLEXIC CHILD

Parent Tips

- Accept the learning difference.
- Do not be overprotective. Do not over-sacrifice.

- Encourage curiosity. For example, if your child is interested in art, trains or model airplanes get involved. This builds stronger relationships.
- Talk honestly with your child.
- Develop self-esteem, worth and competence.
- Do not do for your child what they can do for themselves.
- Set reasonable goals. Do not make things too easy.
- Think long term.
- Be aware of problems associated with dyslexia such as confusion regarding the time of day, where things have been left and following instructions.
- Manage time effectively.
- Be patient.
- Educate yourself about learning difficulties.
- Keep a master file of reports, schoolwork and personal observations.
- Help your child become organised.
- Provide resources and be there at homework time.
- Monitor homework and school progress.
- Provide alternative learning opportunities.
- Read to, with and for your child.
- Praise often and be positive about academic work.
- Arrange appropriate help in and out of school.

Dyslexia Fact Sheet

- *Definition*: Dyslexia has various definitions, but one descriptive and useful one is that it is an *unexpected delay in reading and/or writing*. The delay is unexpected because the person is able in many areas, such as communicating ideas orally, visual reasoning (e.g. seeing how parts fit, construction/assembly) and usually maths. Dyslexia is fundamentally a problem of processing the printed word – a phonological, or sound symbol, fault. Dyslexia is not due to social disadvantage, hearing/vision problems, faulty education or lack of general intelligence.

- *Course*: Dyslexia is life-long, although when assessed and treated early the prognosis is more favourable.
- *Onset*: Teachers, parents and other professionals may suspect a reading/writing problem around senior infants or first class when children are first expected to read and develop a reading vocabulary. At this time, some children (see note on prevalence below) may memorise words (e.g. cat), but when faced with similar looking words (e.g. hat), will not have the phonic awareness to pronounce them. Writing and spelling may also be delayed. Other common problems include letter reversals (e.g. 'p' for 'q'), mispronunciations of similar looking words (e.g. 'that', 'then', 'this' and 'them'), a slow reading rate, difficulty organising thoughts in written form, omissions/additions of words during reading and dysfluency (slow, hesitant and laboured reading).
- *Prevalence*: Thought to be one in every ten children. This is a very high prevalence, if one considers that for every one hundred children, ten will be dyslexic.
- *Cause*: Unknown at present. It is presumed to be due to the brain area which processes phonemes (the connection between letters and sounds that define how we read and spell words).
- *The measurement of dyslexia*: An educational psychological assessment includes measures of intelligence, attainment and other selected tests. The main criteria defining dyslexia are:

    o   A WISC-IV full scale or GAI score in the average band and statistically greater than one or more specific areas of attainment – basic reading, reading comprehension, spelling or written expression attainment (fundamental)
    o   Maths attainment greater than basic reading, reading comprehension and/or spelling (optional)

- *Treatment*: Treatment is multi-faceted and includes specialised reading teaching, school resource support, educational adjustments (e.g. exemption from studying the Irish language, exam concessions) and other suggestions as relevant.
- *Important contacts*: (see References/Contacts)

General Tips

- Consider a brief amount (ten minutes) of reading/spelling/ writing/maths practice four days a week. Include a one-sentence written news item and have at hand a pocket dictionary. Regular practice during school holidays is strongly recommended.
- Source reading materials from Barrington–Stoke, a publishing house that specialises in reading materials for children with reading difficulties (www.barringtonstoke.co.uk).
- Consider phonic-based workbooks (e.g. Toe by Toe).
- Consider joining your local chapter of the Dyslexia Association of Ireland.

****

This next set of recommendations is provided to the parents of a child with a dual diagnosis of AD/HD and ODD; the first set of recommendations pertains to AD/HD and the second to ODD.

****

PARENT MANAGEMENT OF AD/HD AND ODD

AD/HD Facts

What Is AD/HD?

AD/HD stands for attention deficit/hyperactivity disorder. It is a diagnosis usually made during early childhood and it affects about 3 to 5 per cent of the population. It is one of the most common reasons that parents and teachers seek professional child guidance. Children with AD/HD are unable to engage in age-expected behaviours related to concentration and completing academic work, or an excessive amount of other behaviours (e.g. unable to wait, can't relax, always on the go). The general public often describe children with the disorder as bold, lazy or spoiled. AD/HD is really two disorders in one title. Children can either have AD, HD or both.

Attention deficit (AD) is one subset of the condition; children with AD:

- Are inattentive
- Have difficulty completing tasks (leave things unfinished)
- Are easily distracted
- Don't seem to listen when spoken to
- Resist activities which require sustained concentration/mental work
- Constantly move from one activity to another
- Are disorganised
- Regularly lose things
- Are forgetful

Hyperactivity disorder (HD) is the second subset; children with HD:

- Are always on the go
- Have difficulty remaining seated when it is expected
- Are fidgety and squirmy
- Have difficulty relaxing and are restless
- Are impatient – they can't wait, constantly interrupt and intrude, and butt in when it is inappropriate to do so

Children can present with attention deficit, or inattentive presentation, without hyperactivity. Vice versa, children can present with hyperactive–impulsive behaviour but not show any signs of inattention. Children who present with both sets of behaviours have AD/HD – combined presentation.

The above difficulties tend to emerge around the onset of formal schooling. These problems tend to be temperamental features of the child rather than fleeting qualities. Furthermore, the problems tend to exist across people and situations (home and school).

What Causes AD/HD?

The exact cause of AD/HD is unknown at present. However, leading authorities believe that the condition is genetic and that what is inherited is a bio-chemical fault in neuro-transmitters (the nerves which transmit information in the central nervous system).

Course/Development of AD/HD

AD/HD is not outgrown. If not detected and treated, children with the disorder are at risk of (a) early school leaving, (b) substance abuse, (c) criminal behaviour (if conduct disorder is present) and (d) volatile and frequent changes in relationships. The condition typically persists into adulthood, and can result in occupational and relationship difficulties. Depression and other problems may emerge from chronic frustration at not being able to achieve goals.

How Is AD/HD Treated?

A multi-method treatment approach is suggested, one which includes medical management, an individualised educational plan, and support and training for parents. Other treatments are indicated depending on the existence of co-existing difficulties (e.g. speech problems).

Parent Management of AD/HD

- Try not to respond in automatic ways to conflict. Avoid the temptation to yell, scream, nag, lecture, etc. Try to react differently (e.g. by ignoring bad behaviour).
- Let minor battles go.
- Spend quality time with your child. A small amount of daily free time with your child is vital. During this time, do not make demands, nag or question. Instead, follow your child's desires and praise them regularly.
- If you make requests of your child, ensure they complete it. Do not repeat requests over and over; instead, develop a system where you make the request once, provide ample time for it to be completed, and then praise vigorously if it is done. If not, repeat once, then provide a gestural prompt (a movement of the arm/body signalling a direction or area where the task can start, or pointing to the child and the area in succession). Do not get angry or raise your voice. Be matter of fact. Do not make requests and not follow through. If the request is not followed, after a verbal and gestural signal, note (on a diary or recording form)

that the instruction was not complied with. This note could be part of a larger reward system in which compliance earns points toward a desired reward and non-compliance means that points are not accrued.

- All of the educational and behavioural needs of a child should not be the sole responsibility of the mother. Make sure that dads are sharing their responsibility regarding parenting (e.g. attending school meetings, supervising homework).
- Set up situations where your child is around family members who are structured and organised, and who complete tasks. The child may model these qualities.
- Reduce non-productive activities (e.g. too much sleeping, television). Provide one or two weekly structured activities (e.g. horseback riding, soccer).
- Make sure your child gets enough exercise and outdoor recreation.
- Ensure they follow healthy eating habits.
- Supervise your child when possible (e.g. at clubs and during outdoor play).
- Encourage talents and interests. Look for skill areas (e.g. making things, sports) and nurture them.
- Be structured and keep to a routine.
- Learn effective discipline techniques (e.g. praise the positive). When very negative behaviours occur, be quick to enforce time-outs or loss of privileges. Consider whether your child can perform the behaviour you desire. If not, spend time teaching them. Be an empathic parent (i.e. listen to your child, don't talk *at* them).
- Try to determine if your child can do the skill requested (e.g. complete a task), but chooses not to (known as non-compliance) *or* cannot consistently do the skill (known as incompetence). AD/HD is not purposeful opposition. It is the erratic, variable and inconsistent application of skills which lead to problems.
- Give frequent and consistent rewards. AD/HD children need more immediate feedback than other children. Also, realise that

AD/HD children receive more negative feedback than positive compared to other children, so try to redress the balance.

- Use response cost programmes – where the child earns points for good behaviours and loses points for inappropriate behaviour. Set the ratio as five to one: the child earns five points for appropriate behaviour and loses one for inappropriate behaviour.
- Develop a prevention approach – know what situations are high risk for your child and avoid them or make allowances by reducing requests and/or expectations.
- Be educated about AD/HD. Read as much as possible and understand the disorder thoroughly.
- Take care of yourself – you cannot help your child if you do not look after your own physical and mental health needs.
- Consider joining the Irish National Council of AD/HD Support Groups (INCADDS) and HADD Ireland.

Oppositional Defiant Disorder

As discussed in Chapter 4, the main feature of oppositional defiant disorder is a proclivity towards anger, irritability, touchiness, stubbornness, non-compliance, refusal to except blame, and a persistent testing of the limits of an authority (parents, teachers, etc.).

Parent and teacher responses to the problems of oppositional behaviour are typically ineffective (e.g. responding to anger with anger, or completing a task the child should do for him/herself). While there is no easy solution to problems related to oppositional behaviour, the tips below represent a common-sense approach to the problem.

Parent Tips Regarding ODD

- Side-step your child's attempts to engage in negative interactions. Do not respond as usual – look away, change the topic, provide another activity and use a calm voice.
- Use a rational choice method: 'You have two choices. Either you can do X or you can do Y. It is your choice.'

- Allow for expression of feelings, but do not allow verbal abuse or shouting.
- Think of a problem as one with a solution that you and your child can find. Discuss choices and the pros and cons of each. Decide on a plan and follow through on it.
- Search for positives. Oppositional children typically look for negative parent reactions and usually get it. Find a positive element and always point it out to your child (e.g. 'Remember how well you made your bed. You did a really super job').
- Oppositional behaviour is sometimes associated with harsh and inconsistent parent responses to defiant behaviour. Make every effort to avoid these parenting pitfalls.
- Recognise that defiance, anger and demanding behaviour may be a young child's way of communicating their feelings. Thus, rather than responding to the surface behaviour, attempt to see your child's behaviour as a form of communication and a request for connection with you.
- Participate in a structured self-help parenting programme to overcome defiance.
- Know your priorities.
- Act, don't react.
- Perhaps the most common parental pitfall is to continually repeat a request or to nag. Thus, stop repeating comments. The goal is to engage in action but not talk.
- Try to see things from your child's perspective.
- Stop blaming.
- Keep your distance.
- Make consequences (good or bad) immediate.
- Make consequences specific.
- Make consequences consistent.
- Establish incentive programmes before punishment.
- Anticipate and plan for misbehaviour.
- Use a timer with an alarm and set it for a realistic amount of time for your child to complete a given task. If the activity is completed within the agreed time frame, reward your child accordingly. If not, do not punish your child, but also do not provide the reward.

Affirm that there will be another chance to succeed on the next opportunity (perhaps the following day, or later the same day).

- To reduce negative attention-seeking, consider spending quality time with your child in a non-argumentative, positive manner. The activity could be one of mutual interest (e.g. computer games, sport or reading). A specific amount of time (e.g. five minutes) should be set aside on a daily basis where the rule is to be positive and there are no negative comments or emotions. Also, refrain from questioning your child. Quality time could be a reward, again, using a structured programme.

Behaviour Programmes for AD/HD and ODD

Successful behaviour management depends on:

- *Immediacy*: consequences must occur immediately after appropriate/inappropriate behaviour.
- *Contingency*: consequences must occur only for the desired behaviour. If rewards are given when the specific behaviour does not occur, then the effects of management are lessened.
- *Potency*: rewards and behaviour reduction methods should be truly desirable or undesirable if they are to work. Children disinterested in the consequences will not change their behaviour to obtain or prevent them.

Be prepared for the behaviour challenges a structured management system will create; behaviour may worsen before it dramatically improves. Also, your child may test the system. Therefore, enlist your child's participation from the beginning. If behaviour is difficult as a direct result of the new system, this form of negative behaviour should be treated as any other example of unwarranted behaviour – there should be consequences. It may be useful to use a behaviour contract (see below).

Behaviour Contract

I, <u>Mary</u>, agree to accept the following rules:

- Once I sign this contract, I will not ask my mom/dad about the rules. I will try my best to follow the rules of this contract. If things do not go well, I will accept the result. But I want things to go well so I can do fun things.
- The contract will be in place each evening when I get home from school until I go to bed.
- I will do the following:

  - If I want a drink, I will get it myself; same with snacks.
  - If I want something and my mom says 'no' I will not cry or have a tantrum. I will not ask for it again.
  - I will complete twenty minutes of homework each day without temper or upset.

- If I do all of the three things above, I will get a special treat at the end of the evening (to be agreed with parents).
- If I do not do the three things, I will not get a special treat. However, I can try again tomorrow.

(Individualise with Mary in the drawing up of the rules of the contract.)

I, _____ agree to provide the above special treat in accordance with this contract
(Parent Name)

We have read and reviewed the terms of this contract and agree to it. The contract will be re-designed as necessary.
Signed: _____   _____
       (Child)   (Parent)

- With regards to non-compliance, keep tasks brief and be realistic.
- Try to limit requests to a standard list of three or four items. For example, 'brush your teeth and get ready for bed' would be two. Along with Mary, standardise a core set of compliance activities. Compliance with parent requests could be part of a more general reward system.
- Make high-preference activities contingent on completion of low-preference tasks. For example, access to a computer will only be provided contingent on completion of a daily/specific task. This will mean limiting unrestricted access to rewarding activities.
- Build a positive attitude by 'catching' good behaviour – see below.

Paying Attention to Positive Behaviour

Rationale

When children have behaviour difficulties, parents spend a great deal of time reprimanding (e.g. 'Don't do that') and providing corrective feedback (e.g. 'You didn't pick up your clothes'). More and more time is spent in the negative cycle of problem behaviour–negative response. Good behaviour is ignored because it is expected while difficult behaviour usually gets parent attention. This programme offers an alternative approach. Even the most disruptive child will behave appropriately at times and we must train ourselves to look at and respond to good behaviour as well as problem behaviour. THIS PROGRAMME IS EASY TO READ BUT NOT SO EASY TO DO.

Method

Consider the positive aspects of behaviour your child exhibits – what they enjoy doing (indoor and outdoor activities). During high-risk times (e.g. playing with siblings, mealtimes), make a concerted effort to re-train your attention to positive behaviour, even if it occurs for small periods. You may need to make reminder cards and post them in high-profile areas of the house at first in order to make the awareness of positive behaviour more conscious. When your child is behaving appropriately (e.g. not bothering you, playing appropriately, doing schoolwork), stop what you are doing and provide *positive feedback* like:

- 'I really like the way you are playing so nicely.'
- 'What a good boy/girl you are for letting me talk on the phone without disturbing me.'

Be positive, genuine and expressive when providing praise. Go to wherever the child is engaging in good behaviour (e.g. the sitting room, outside) in order to praise them. After providing positive feedback, immediately return to what you are doing. For very difficult children, you may need to focus on good behaviour every two or three minutes. You can gradually increase the time periods between positive attention and set a maximum time based on your child's needs.

Sometimes parents may wish to purposely watch their child during play activity. You can engage in another activity in the same room or, in some cases, may wish to narrate your child's activities (as a commentator would). If you narrate, *ask no questions and give no commands*. Just describe what the child is doing at all times. Occasionally provide *positive feedback* about what you like that the child is doing (e.g. 'I like it when you play quietly' or 'I like it when you don't throw toys').

Whenever misbehaviour occurs in your presence or during times when you are undertaking this programme, try to *ignore it*. For example, if you are playing with your child and he/she throws a toy, turn away and attend to something else in the room. If misbehaviour escalates, leave the room and return later when your child is behaving more appropriately. Each parent should spend at least fifteen to twenty minutes with the child each day with this programme in mind.

A Structured System for Requests

Use a structured and systematic approach to giving requests, such as the three-step guided prompt system described below.

Three Types of Prompts

- *Verbal*: Orally state your request (e.g. 'Mary, come back to the table'). If the child does not comply within five or ten seconds, give a gestural prompt.
- *Gestural*: Repeat your request and include a gestural prompt (e.g. point to the child and to the place you want them to go or the object you want them to pick up). If the child does not comply within five or ten seconds, give a physical prompt.
- *Physical*: Give a gentle touch or light direction of body in the direction of the area/object you want them to attend to. A physical prompt is not a harsh or physically aggressive response, such as pushing, slapping or using an overly firm grasp. If the physical prompt leads to a tantrum or physical stand-off, let it go and wait for next task. Also, with older children, some parents may wish to do only verbal and gestural prompts and leave out the physical prompt.

How to Use Prompts

Prompts should be simple, one-step requests (e.g. 'Mary, take your plate to the sink'). Multiple-step requests like 'clean your room' or 'get undressed' should be avoided because they are too difficult and too long. Instead of 'clean your room', ask your child to put away one object at a time (e.g. 'put the truck in the box'). In a single day you will give numerous requests, and you should use whatever method you want for *all of the requests except the one area you want to standardise*. The one you choose for three-step guided compliance will have a certain 'staged' feel to it. You want that effect. Also, it is important to *use the same requests each day*.

Consistently use the procedure for doing verbal, gestural or physical prompts: make a verbal request, wait five seconds, then give a gestural prompt, wait five seconds, then give a physical prompt. Only praise your child if they comply with a verbal or gestural prompt. Remember, *physical prompts should be done without force*.

There will be situations where a parent has to respond to very negative behaviour, such as physical aggression to a peer/parent, property destruction (breaking toys/furniture) or cursing at parents. These behaviours cannot be ignored and require immediate action. In these situations, parents require an emergency response. There-fore, consider the quiet time procedure.

Quiet Time Procedure

Quiet time means that the child is placed in a situation where they cannot get positive (or negative) rewards or attention. During this time, the child must remain quiet and calm for a specified time period. Quiet time is a highly effective method for reducing problem behav-iours, especially aggression, defiance and temper tantrums. Quiet time is used when the negative behaviour cannot be ignored. It is most effective when used in conjunction with positive methods when positive behaviours occur (e.g. praise for complying with a request).

Explain to your child what behaviours result in quiet time (you may have to model the behaviour so that the child will have a clear picture of it). Also specify where in the house quiet time will take place (e.g. in a certain chair or particular place) and how long it will be (a general rule of thumb is one minute for every year of the child's age – so two minutes for a two-year-old, three for a three-year-old, etc.; it should never be longer than five minutes). A good quiet time area is well-lit, free from dangerous objects and away from television, toys or other desired objects. Usually quiet time is in an adult-sized chair in a corner or hallway. The first few quiet time attempts are the most difficult. Children may kick, scream or cry. If your child remains in the seat, allow these behaviours but do not pay any non-verbal or verbal attention to them. If your child leaves the seat, you must return him/her to the seat. You may have to repeat this several times. If you do so consistently and without emotion and remain calm, your child will learn to stay seated for the allotted period.

Practice quiet time before using it (emphasise to your child that this practice is pretend). The key points to using quiet time are:

- Use quiet time consistently.
- When the problem behaviour occurs, tell your child what he/she did and say 'go to quiet time please'. If your child does not go, give them a minimally physical prompt towards the quiet time area. Ignore any crying and apologies from your child. Do not talk with your child and do not reprimand them. Be quiet and look straight ahead.
- When your child is in quiet time, do not talk or look at him/her.
- Have a timer nearby. Set it for the agreed upon time (between two and five minutes). Do not start the timer until the child is quiet and calm. If, after you start the timer, the child becomes upset and cries, re-set the timer for an additional minute.
- If your child continues to engage in the inappropriate behaviour then re-set the timer for one more minute and repeat the procedure. Continue to do so until the child calms down.
- When the quiet time is over, ask, 'Are you ready to get up?' Your child must say 'yes' or nod. If the child says 'no', re-set the timer for another minute.
- Following quiet time quickly look for and praise positive behaviour from your child. Remember to catch your child being good more often when employing quiet time.

****

Below is a summary of an individualised plan for six-year-old Mary. This programme illustrates some of the earlier noted points.

****

INDIVIDUALISED BEHAVIOUR PROGRAMME FOR MARY

- Pick two or three high-priority specific requests (e.g. 'Brush your teeth'). Make sure a request like 'get ready for bed' has clear component parts (e.g. 'put on your pyjamas and get into bed', or whatever sub-tasks are identified). Then employ the methods mentioned previously. For more complex requests, such as 'do your homework', three-step guided compliance will not be relevant.

- When Mary cries/screams/complains, make a concerted effort to engage in planned ignoring.
- Always seek to randomly praise any degree of appropriate play with Mary, even partial compliance with a request.
- The most important parent behaviour is not acquiescing to Mary's demands during a rage episode. If you succumb to her rage, it will increase the intensity and frequency of tantrums. It will also make it very difficult to fix the existing problem.
- As discussed, the general assignment is trying something different. The area/time selected was dinner and that the parents will cease feeding Mary. Mary is a capable primary-school-aged child who can feed herself. Discuss with Mary the new rules about independence (i.e. feeding herself). Explain the new procedure that food will be provided and Mary can feed herself and that if she does not eat the food provided, there will be no other opportunities for snacks later in the evening. More than likely, Mary will leave the table and think that she can access snacks later. This will require careful planning (i.e. making sure food is unavailable when the meal is finished). Also, Mary will likely have a severe tantrum when food is not provided. Again, explain all this clearly beforehand. If Mary tantrums, ignore her and seek to distance yourself from her anger. Eventually, the tantrum will conclude and the opportunity for food is available the next morning.
- Aim to *not* demonstrate the emotional reactions (e.g. frustration, anger) that you do not want Mary to display.
- Be very vigilant with regards to Mary's faulty cognitive thinking. Occasionally, children use extreme words such as 'always' or 'never'. If these words are used, simply repeat the word in a questioning manner (e.g. 'I always ...?', 'You never ...?') and do so several times to indicate the fallacy of Mary's perceptions.

Interventions for Mary

Cognitive behavioural therapy (CBT) is recommended. CBT is a method of psychological intervention in which the therapist engages a child in self-exploration as to how thinking, emotions and behaviours are linked. There are a variety of methods a therapist will use to help the child learn more about the interconnectedness of feelings, thoughts and actions. The specific techniques used depend on the type of problem (e.g. anxiety, anger) and the age of the child.

****

REVIEW ASSESSMENT

The final aspect of a report will often make a recommendation for ongoing monitoring and/or a complete review (all data re-collected). A review assessment is essential, especially for younger children. Only through a repeat evaluation can progress be gauged. A standard review recommendation is given below.

****

REVIEW

Ongoing monitoring and full re-assessment in 24 months is recommended.

****

A RESOURCE TEACHER'S PERSPECTIVE

My present position is as a resource teacher. I have been a learning support teacher, classroom teacher and teaching principal. Over the years, I have taught children with different special educational needs.

When children experience learning difficulties with various parts of the curriculum, we can sometimes provide support within the school. This is known as learning support and is helpful when teachers observe a child struggling with the beginning aspects of reading, writing, maths and language. In these cases, we usually try to provide support without referring to a psychologist, or other professional, for an assessment.

Despite learning support and the efforts of parents and teachers to assist a child, there may be other difficulties that impede academic and social progress: a child may be very inattentive and easily distracted; the same child may be very active and talkative and cannot seem to stay on task or stay seated for long. A child may have difficulty relating to other children and act in a way that makes it difficult for him or her to be part of the class group.

Sometimes learning support is not enough. Sometimes, a parent may feel a child should obtain learning support but we cannot provide it based on school test results that do not indicate a significant problem. In these cases, we often advise parents that a psychoeducational assessment would be of benefit. This can lead to various parent reactions, such as disappointment and fear and perhaps lack of understanding as to what an assessment will mean for their child. In some cases, parents will not wish to pursue an assessment and we continue to provide assistance as best we can.

When parents do not wish to have their child assessed, a learning support teacher may not be able to fully address a child's needs, particularly in the areas of concentration, listening, self-management, organisation and social development. The child may continue to experience difficulty in the classroom and require frequent prompts and reprimands to stay on task; this is disruptive to the whole class and does not encourage positive self-esteem.

One recent case that comes to mind is a child who, I felt, showed many of the characteristics of AD/HD – he could not sustain concentration, was restless and impulsive, and was greatly underachieving. We were aware of reading difficulties and provided learning support. However, progress was slow and we felt there were behaviour issues that we were not addressing.

We recommended an assessment and the psychologist diagnosed AD/HD. Subsequently, we were able to allocate three hours of weekly resource support for the child. We developed an individual education plan (IEP), which addressed his greatest needs: listening, following directions, organisation and social skills. I can also liaise with the class teacher so that when the child is inattentive during a lesson, the teacher can note this and I can teach the particular concept in the resource context.

Without a psychological assessment, we would not have been able to develop an individual programme for this child. The long-term outcome would certainly be more negative in the absence of an assessment. Unfortunately, I am aware of some parents whom we advised to seek an assessment but who will probably never do so.

Since the inception of resource teaching, the child has made great progress. He seems happier and is now able to keep pace with his classmates. Of course, some difficulties continue, such as distractibility and restlessness, but these problems are not interfering with learning as much as they used to. The parents are very pleased with their child's school progress and achievements.

FINAL COMMENT

The implementation of some recommendations can be difficult and time-consuming. Sometimes there are differences of opinion about the specific remedies; sometimes, it is not always clear whether a student qualifies for a given intervention. The educational supports may take time and further clarification before full, or partial, implementation.

As for specific parent recommendations, changing one's approach to difficult behaviour is not an easy parent task. However, even one or two minor alterations in parent approach, taken from a list of parent recommendations, can be very effective. Some examples of the difference an assessment and change in approach can make:

- Derek showed noticeable improvements in reading subsequent to the provision of learning support in school. Now there is a clear focus on what the problem is and how to address it.
- Maria realises that her child's reading and writing problems are not due to lack of effort, laziness or not paying attention to detail. Rather, she now knows that her daughter has an underlying processing fault with phonics and she is more tolerant and accepting of her daughter's difficulties.
- A change in the language orientation of the school has dramatically improved behaviour issues for Stephen.
- Jessica now recognises her talents and strengths and has learned to focus on her skills.

Some recommendations are administrative and involve the Department of Education. There is a clear system in place and relevant personnel will review the psychologist's report to make the final decision as to what supports are necessary and how these supports will be provided. In situations where an assessment reveals an obvious problem, the inevitable outcome is almost universally positive. There is now a clear explanation and methods to address the problem.

Overall, it is hoped that the benefits of an assessment are clear from this chapter. With the many advances in knowledge and technology, there are a variety of solutions which can be implemented once an assessment is complete.

7

Conclusion

Let's return to the question that is the focus of this book: Does my child need help? Using the categories presented in Chapter 4, the first step in answering this question is to consider the different areas of your child's development. For example, learning and language represent one distinct area of functioning. A second area would be attention and concentration, since the ability to focus and stay on task is paramount for success in school and work. Physical and motor development, particularly gross (large muscle movements – running, walking, catching a ball, etc.) and fine (smaller muscle movements involved in grip and manipulation of objects) motor skills are also relevant to school progress. Social interaction skills are apparent from an early age and are an integral part of school. The emotional/behavioural world of a child is an essential part of development. Finally, how do children appraise themselves, since self-evaluation is the basis for self-esteem?

Across these six areas, you may worry about your child's ability in one or more domains. Worry and concern lead to the natural process of gathering more information, such as observing your child, comparing him or her with other children, talking to friends and family about your concern, and further reading about the topic. From this information gathering, you may feel that your concern is minimal, or that the problem is fleeting, and, therefore, need not take any further action. Or, after gathering information, you may continue to feel that the problem is substantial and the cause of significant distress to your child. If this is the case, it is advisable to discuss your concerns with your child's teacher. If the problem is not considered significant in school, you may feel justified in not pursuing the issue any further. However, if the school is also cognisant of problems, or if you still feel there is an issue, even when it is not considered significant in the school context, you are well advised to seek a professional assessment. This decision-making process is illustrated in Figure 7.1.

Having read this book, it is hoped that you will be in a better position to decide on whether to pursue an assessment by fully understanding the process and methods which are typically used in evaluation. The methods of collecting information integral to the assessment are detailed in Chapters 2 and 3. The outcomes of an assessment are given in Chapter 4. In Chapter 5, a sample of a written report is provided. Finally, in Chapter 6, the typical recommendations of a psychologist are outlined. This information will help you decide whether a psychologist's assessment could be of benefit to your child.

It is further hoped that some of the common misconceptions about assessments (e.g. labelling) are dispelled by this book and that parents recognise that an assessment will only benefit their child. Some of the many benefits of assessment include:

- The child will recognise his/her personal strengths and weaknesses.
- If a problem is detected, the child, parent and teacher can better understand the issue and stop making incorrect inferences. For example, a parent and/or teacher might attribute numerous spelling mistakes to carelessness when, in fact, the child is dyslexic and their poor spelling is a symptom of that. Likewise, children might view themselves as 'slow', 'stupid' or 'dumb', or use other negative self-statements. If their problem is specific to an area of the curriculum (e.g. reading, writing or maths), then it is likely that their overall ability is normal, even above the normal range, and this scientific evidence can be fed back to the child so a more accurate self-appraisal is formed (e.g. 'I am smart but have a specific problem with spelling').
- Once the outcomes are known, an individualised plan can be put in place to address any clear weaknesses. Part of this plan will include several of the recommendations covered in Chapter 6.

Figure 7.1: How to Decide if Your Child Needs Help

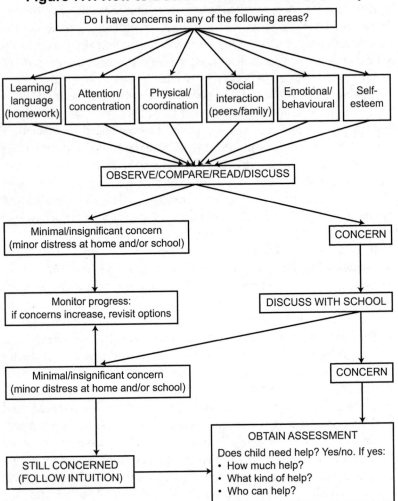

As is clear from the parents and special educational teachers who contributed their experiences to this book, an assessment is vital to the educational and psychological development of the child. Subsequent to an assessment, parents report very positive changes in their child's attitude to and behaviour regarding school. Recall Adrian from

Chapter 1, who was angry and irritable before school, but after psychological assessment is now agreeable and far easier to manage. In Chapter 4, his parents described Paul as very distracted and aggressive towards other children. Once his problems were categorised, a specific educational plan was put in place to address their child's needs. In Chapter 5 we met Francis, who considered himself 'stupid', basing his self-appraisal entirely on poor reading ability. Once Francis understood that he was 'smart' and that his difficulty with reading was a specific problem, he adjusted his academic self-image and was far happier and content.

Once assessed, teachers and schools can individualise the curriculum and provide necessary supports for a child with clear needs. These can include extra teaching support, language exemptions, exam accommodations, a special needs assistant, assistive technology, inclusion in a special class/unit, other professional assessments/interventions, an individual educational plan, and recommendations for managing learning and behaviour at home.

Without a doubt, an educational psychologist's assessment can be instrumental to a child's education. The results will indicate whether a problem is evident, what kind and to what degree, and, of course, what can be done to address the identified problem. Children, parents and teachers will have increased understanding and awareness of the issue, which is fundamental to ensuring the best possible outcome.

Hopefully, after reading this book, potential fears and misconceptions about an assessment have been replaced with the knowledge that an assessment represents a win–win situation. The most important question – 'Does my child need help?' – will be answered. If help is required, a plan will be developed which can empower parents, teachers and children to take steps toward progress and improvement.

References and Contacts

Official Documents

The Department of Education circular relevant to the diagnostic categories in Chapter 4 is Circular 08/02. You can find this circular by going to www.education.ie/en/Schools-Colleges/Services/Teacher-Allocations-Staffing/Circular-08-02-Information-Note.pdf.

To learn more about the Disability Access Route to Education visit the website at http://accesscollege.ie/dare/index.php.

Forms similar to the 'Parent Information' and 'Referral Form' discussed in Chapter 2 can be found on www.education.ie/en/Schools-Colleges/Services/Educational-Psychologist-NEPS-/NEPS-SCPA-Referral-Form.pdf.

The National Council for Special Education (NCSE) Working Group proposal regarding a new system for allocating resource teachers can be found at http://www.ncse.ie/uploads/1/NCSE_Booklet_webFINAL_10_06_14.pdf.

Specific References in the Text

American Psychiatric Association (2013) *Diagnostic and Statistical Manual of Mental Disorders* (fifth edition), Washington DC: American Psychiatric Association.
Sattler, Jerome M. (1988) *Assessment of Children* (third edition), San Diego, CA: Jerome M. Sattler Publisher Inc.

Sattler, Jerome M. (2014) *Foundations of Behavioural, Social, and Clinical Assessment of Children* (sixth edition), San Diego, CA: Jerome M. Sattler Publisher Inc.

Wechsler Individual Achievement Test (second edition) (2005), London: Pearson Clinical.

Wechsler Individual Scale of Intelligence (fourth edition) (2004), London: Pearson Clinical.

Wilkinson, William K. (2003) *Straight Talk about Attention Deficit/ Hyperactivity Disorder: A Guide for Irish Parents and Professionals*, Cork: Collins Press.

NATIONAL DISABILITY ORGANISATIONS

Asperger Syndrome Association of Ireland: www.aspireireland.ie, 01 878 0027

Dyslexia Association of Ireland: www.dyslexia.ie, 01 877 6001. From their website, you can locate your local branch. This website also has information on dyscalculia.

Dyspraxia Association of Ireland: www.dyspraxia.ie, 01-8747085

HADD Ireland (for people affected by attention deficit/hyperactivity disorder (AD/HD)): www.hadd.ie, 01 874 8349

Irish Autism Action: www.autismireland.ie, 044 937 1680

Irish National Council of AD/HD Support Groups: www.incadds. ie, 091 755 090